DNA by Dennis Kelly:
Routes to Revision

DNA by Dennis Kelly:
Routes to Revision

written by Iona Towler-Evans

OBERON BOOKS
LONDON

WWW.OBERONBOOKS.COM

First published in 2017 by Oberon Books Ltd

521 Caledonian Road, London N7 9RH

Tel: +44 (0) 20 7607 3637 / Fax: +44 (0) 20 7607 3629

e-mail: info@oberonbooks.com

www.oberonbooks.com

PB ISBN: 9781786821171

E ISBN: 9781786821188

Designed by Konstantinos Vasdekis

Printed, bound and converted
by CPI Group (UK) Ltd, Croydon, CR0 4YY.

Visit www.oberonbooks.com to read more about all our books and to buy them. You will also find features, author interviews and news of any author events, and you can sign up for e-newsletters so that you're always first to hear about our new releases.

Contents

Introduction

Remember: This is a play to be performed

This is not a novel, this is a piece of theatre – it only comes alive when it is performed. You can't understand it unless you have been inside it as if you are the characters, which is why tasks have been designed for you. These tasks will enable you to begin to see the situation from the characters' point of view. You will examine contrasting perspectives on an event. I have talked to the author, Dennis Kelly, so you can also look at the play from the author's point of view. As an audience member or reader, you may have another point of view which differs from that of the author and the characters. We have to be aware of all these perspectives when we study the play and this isn't difficult. When you watch television, you imagine the points of view of the characters – you are on the outside looking in. This guide, I hope, will place you on the inside, at times in the 'shoes of the characters', walking around exploring the action (at least in your head). It aims to show how the characters give you an insight into the playwright's point of view, and the themes in the play, plus the impact they both have on the audience's perspective.

Strategies which help you appreciate the playwright's use of theatrical devices

The playwright employs a range of theatrical devices, one of which is the dramatic tension created between characters, achieved in various ways. Another is their use of structural devices and their use of language reflected via a group of contrasting characters.

The play *DNA* was new to me, so after reading it, I took the opportunity to find out more about it by seeing young people of your age working on a performance of selected extracts for their GCSE Drama examination. These performers have kindly agreed for me to use some of their photographs from their rehearsals. Sometimes their views of the characters differed – the result of experimenting with the text as if they were the characters, and experiencing the tension between them at certain points. You might like to try out some of the strategies they found helpful, either on your own or with a friend.

Tasks which enable you to arrive at your own personal response and interpretation

When I thought about creating this guide, it occurred to me that it ought to include a number of tasks which you could engage in as a way of developing your own understanding of the play and, more importantly, your own interpretation and personal response to it. So I have included a number of tasks, including the photographs which form a particular task for you to work on.

What the examiner is looking for

Often, we lose sight of what an examiner is looking for in the answer to a question and in the grade they will give the student. I have tried my best to illustrate this as we go along, so each task is related to key assessment criteria. The aim of this guide is to make you think, not copy, so that you arrive at your own view of the play and its features. The playwright himself, Dennis Kelly, believes that 'young people like to think' and we hope this guide will help you to raise questions about the play, *DNA*, its themes and its meanings. You may wish to start at the beginning, but there are other starting points. You may prefer to begin with what Dennis Kelly says about the play – although his views are woven into various sections – or you may want to remind yourself of the plot, or the characters. Wherever you choose to start, I hope you will find the tasks engaging and helpful in preparing you for your examination. Good luck!

Iona Towler-Evans

1

A Way of Looking at a Play

**When you last played a computer game
were you thinking about how it was designed?**

Probably not; you were probably just enjoying the game. Designers of computer games take us on a journey. We might meet a monster, a dragon, and find ourselves in a dungeon. There, we could come across obstacles from which we hope to be rescued but we might be in danger of meeting another monster. Just as the computer game designer puts the game together as a structure, a playwright creates a structure for us as an audience to respond to. The computer game designer usually gives us a choice of options to follow, unlike the playwright whose creation has mapped out the journey for us.

It's not about whether you liked it or not

For the purposes of an examination question, we have to go beyond simply enjoying the experience of watching a play. We have to be cleverer than that: we need to know how the play was created and written, how it was designed and constructed and its overall effect – not whether or not we liked it.

The playwright's intentions and our responses

The playwright will have their reasons for writing and constructing the play in the way they choose, and you will have your responses to it – but their reasons and your responses may be different, of course. As Dennis Kelly himself suggests, once the play is performed in public, it is out of his control, and you may discover ideas he hasn't actually intended or considered. For example, Kelly says of *DNA* that 'it is not a play about bullying.' As far as he is concerned, the bullying has already happened, before the play starts. You of course may interpret some of the episodes differently and find ones where bullying exists.

The playwright's perspective

Whatever Kelly's intentions and whatever our response, we need to be mindful that he structured the play in a particular way and for particular purpose and effect. He designed characters to live in the locations in his play, for the period of the play. They are all different, some speak more than others, some listen more than others, some are leaders and others followers. Kelly uses a range of devices to create meaning for the audience, and pose questions for them as well as for himself as a writer.

With reference to the play, *DNA*, Kelly provides us with the following insight:

'The question is how far will we go to save the group? When I write a play I don't have an answer. I think about a question I don't have an answer to – there's never an easy answer as this makes it more interesting although the play does pose this moral question.'

Therefore, the play is always more than it seems, and this revision guide will hopefully help you uncover the meanings it holds for you.

2

Assessment Objectives (AOs) Explained

What examiners are looking for when you write about this play

For this essay, there are 30 available marks. There are, however, an additional 4 marks for spelling, punctuation and grammar.

This essay question will appear on Paper 2, which is called 'Modern Texts and Poetry'. The *DNA* question will be in Section A of the paper. You will have a choice of 2 questions on *DNA*, of which you answer only 1.

You will be assessed in 4 areas. The areas for assessment are called 'Assessment Objectives' (AOs). Below they are explained, with the number of marks allocated to each one.

AO1: (12 marks)

Read, understand and respond to texts.

For this, you should be able to demonstrate:

- Your own ideas and understanding of the text

- An informed personal response

- An ability to illustrate your points by using textual reference

Put simply, this AO assesses your understanding of the characters and themes in the text and your ability to support your ideas.

AO2: (12 marks)

Analyze the language, form and structure used by a writer to create meanings and effects, using relevant subject terminology where appropriate.

In other words, this means how well you back up what you have said in AO1, by explaining the effects of the writer's methods, using subject terminology.

AO3: (6 marks)

Show understanding of the relationships between texts and the contexts in which they were written, such as:

- The context in which the text was written (social/historical context)

- The context within which the text is set (location)

(Context may refer to social structures and features/cultural contexts/periods in time as well as literary contexts, such as genres.)

Put simply, this is the way you can relate what you have said in the previous AOs to various contexts. You can be flexible in your contextual references, referring to historical/social/political/literary influences or to the effect of genre. In the case of the play *DNA*, you may consider its particular genre as a play for the theatre designed for young people, and/or you may make reference to the use of settings and locations, for that particular audience.

3

A Summary of *DNA* by Dennis Kelly

A group of teenagers do something bad, which they think is really bad, then panic and cover the whole thing up. But their plans to cover up become complicated and put pressure on the group, from which emerge leaders, followers and consequences.

Act 1

Scene 1 (A Street)
Jan and Mark. Mark is questioned by Jan regarding the news that someone is 'dead' and this throws the audience into the centre of their crisis.

Scene 2 (A Field)
Leah and Phil. Leah talks and Phil eats an ice-cream. Leah speaks throughout and appears to speak for Phil who remains silent.

Scene 3 (A Wood)
Lou, John Tate and Danny. John Tate tries to take control of the group by using fear and threats confrontation. He bans others from using the word 'dead'. Richard threatens his leadership but this is suppressed. When Mark and Jan arrive (with Leah and Phil) they explain to the group their version of events leading up to Adam falling into the grille. They try to justify their vicious attack on him by saying he was laughing. Phil finally speaks and devises a plan to frame a non-existent person.

Scene 4 (A Field)
Leah delivers what appears to be a monologue about bonobos being our nearest relatives: **'Chimps are evil. They murder each other... They kill and sometimes torture each other to find a better position within the social structure'** (page 26). This could be seen as the playwright's voice coming through about the nature of groups and how far we go to protect our own position within them.

Act 2

Scene 1 (A Street)
The audience learns from Jan and Mark that someone is 'not going' – this is a reference to Brian not going to the police station.

Scene 2 (A Field)
Leah is still trying to elicit a response from Phil. She talks about the nature of happiness. She shows him a Tupperware container and says it is Jerry. She describes how she has killed him.

Scene 3 (A Wood)
The plan has gone wrong. Because Cathy used her 'initiative' to find a man that fits the description that Phil invented, the police have now found the man that matched that description. Brian at first refuses to go into the police station to identify the man who is being framed. Phil threatens him with being taken up to the grille if he doesn't go. Finally, Brian goes.

Scene 4 (A Field)
Leah continues to talk to Phil and he fails to respond until the end of the scene where he says one word. In this scene, Leah claims to experience *déjà vu*.

Act 3

Scene 1 (A Street)

Mark reveals to Jan that Cathy has 'found someone' in the woods. It turns out to be Adam.

Scene 2 (A Field)

Phil is preparing to eat a waffle when Leah arrives in the scene with a packed suitcase. She seems to be trying to gain Phil's attention by threatening to leave and telling him not to try and stop her... but he doesn't. She tells him about Adam's memorial and that she has seen Cathy on the TV. She tells him that everyone is happier: **'Funny thing is they're all actually behaving better as well'** (page 47).

Scene 3 (A Wood)

Adam is alive and appears torn and dirty – he has been living in a hedge. He has survived by living off dead animals. He has clearly sustained a head injury. Brian, who is by this time on medication and behaves in a very childlike way, claims: **'I found him'**. Phil instructs Jan, Mark and Lou to leave and not say anything. He shows Cathy how to kill Adam by tying a plastic bag around Brian's head which Brian accepts as a 'game'. Leah begs him not to do this.

Scene 4 (A Field)

Phil and Leah. The roles seem slightly reversed as this time Leah does not speak. Phil offers her a sweet and he puts his arm round her to show affection, which is the first time we have seen any sign of affection from him. She spits out the sweet and leaves in disgust. Phil calls after her.

Act 4

Scene 1 (A Street)

Mark reveals to Jan that someone has 'gone'. It becomes clear to the audience that this turns out to be Leah.

Scene 2 (A Field)

Richard has replaced Leah, and her role in the group by doing all the talking, in order to connect with Phil. He tries to persuade Phil to re-join the group, but Phil does not speak. For the first time, in this location, he does not eat. Leah's departure seems to have affected him. Richard tells him what has happened to the rest of the group.

A LIST OF CHARACTERS

- MARK
- JAN
- LEAH
- PHIL
- LOU
- JOHN TATE
- DANNY
- RICHARD
- CATHY
- BRIAN
- ADAM

● **AO2:**

Analyze the language used by the writer to create meanings and effects, using relevant subject terminology where appropriate.

Symbol explanation

■ Language

◆ Stage Directions

✦ Meaning of Play

CHARACTER OVERVIEW

We learn about the characters from stage directions (particularly Phil for whom we are given more detail from stage directions), other characters' responses to them especially from inferring from their dialogue and language, and through the descriptions of their actions (e.g., on page 23-24):

Pause. They all stare at LEAH and PHIL.

LEAH goes to say something, but nothing comes out.

Silence.

More silence.

PHIL puts his Coke carefully on the ground.

Mark and Jan

Act 3, Scene 1 (page 44)

Mark and Jan appear on the street together. They act as the 'chorus' or narrators, commenting on the action of the play, while also being part of it. As in the following extract, their conversations keep us up to date with the sequence of events but also bring intrigue to the audience, as the subject of their conversation is not always disclosed at the outset:

MARK: Yes.

JAN: No, no

MARK: yes

JAN: no. No way, that's

MARK: I know

Act 1, Scene 1 (page 9)

When we first encounter Mark and Jan we are thrown into the middle of the crisis faced by the group. Mark appears to be the one who is more well-informed. He relays the information to Jan, who responds with questions:

JAN: Dead?

MARK: Yeah.

JAN: What, dead?

MARK: Yeah

Act 1, Scene 3 (page 20)

Together, they are responsible for the events surrounding the bullying of Adam that led to him falling into the grille.

> **Their language is often monosyllabic and this contributes to the pace and rhythm of these moments in the play.**

They both try to distance themselves from the tragedy of the event:

MARK: ...I mean we were just having a laugh, weren't we, we were all, you know...

Act 1, Scene 3 (page 22)

■ **The word 'laughing' is repeated throughout the same scene, but is punctuated and contrasted with words such as 'terrified', 'crying', 'stubbed out cigarettes', 'punch him' and 'pegged a stone'.**

While Mark tries to distance himself, by playing down the seriousness of the event, Jan distances herself by being in denial:

MARK: ...we can make him do –

JAN: That's when I went home

MARK: anything, yeah, only because you had to.

JAN: I wasn't there when –

MARK: Only because you had to, you would've been there otherwise, you did all the...

Beat.

Act 1, Scene 3 (page 57)

The group, particularly Jan, look to Phil for reassurance and take instructions from him:

JAN: Are we going to be in trouble.

PHIL: If you go now and say nothing to no one about this, you won't be in trouble.

Act 4, Scene 2 (page 64)

Finally, at the end of the play:

RICHARD: And Jan and Mark have taken up shoplifting, they're really good at it, get you anything you want.

Leah

Act 1, Scene 2 (page 11)

Leah appears in the Field scenes with Phil, in each act, apart from Act 4, by which time she has left.

During these scenes, we see how Leah attempts to communicate with Phil in the hope of gaining a response. For example:

LEAH: ...I mean is it a negative, are you thinking a negative thing about –

Not that I'm bothered. I'm not bothered, Phil, I'm not, it doesn't, I don't care. You know. I don't...

Act 1, Scene 4 (page 26)

Leah is intelligent and imaginative. She often goes off into 'flights of fancy' about her ideas related to other worlds.

➤ **She likes to think about things; her interests extend beyond the other members of the group and certainly offer us connections between the bonobos and chimps and her fellow young people:**

LEAH: Empathy. That's what bonobos have. Amazing really, I mean they're exactly like chimps, but the tiniest change in their DNA... The woman was saying that if we'd discovered bonobos before chimps our understanding of ourselves would be very different.

Pause. PHIL pulls out a bag of crisps.

Act 3, Scene 3 (page 58)

Leah demonstrates perseverance and loyalty – she has known Phil since childhood and looks up to his leadership. She is one of the few characters who shows empathy and is concerned about the individuals within the group, rather than about the group as a whole:

LEAH: It's Adam, Phil, Adam! We used to go to his birthday parties, he used to have that cheap ice cream and we used to take the piss, remember?

Act 1, Scene 2 (page 10)

She tries to solve the group's problems but ultimately turns to Phil to deal with it. By the end of the play, she perhaps realizes that being with Phil compromises her morality.

Her speeches are virtually monologues as there is no response from Phil, and Kelly has devised mainly interrogative sentence types for her character:

LEAH: What are you thinking?

...

Are you thinking about me?

...

What good things? Phil?

Act 1, Scene 2 (pages 11-12)

By using a string of interrogative and rhetorical questions, Leah seems to adopt a stream of consciousness in a long speech:

LEAH: Do I disgust you? I do. No. I do. No don't because, it's alright, its fine...

...

[ending with]

What are you thinking?

Phil

Act 1, Scene 2 (pages 10-12)

The first time we meet Phil he is in the field with Leah. He is eating an ice cream. He is silent throughout Leah's monologue, and there is no stage direction at this point to suggest any non-verbal action, apart from eating.

Act 2, Scene 3 (pages 23-24)

By Act 2, Scene 3 (page 24), the story has been told about the stoning of Adam. At this point, Phil intervenes and the first thing he says in the entire play is an instruction:

> **PHIL: Cathy, Danny, Mark, you go to Adam's house, you wait until his mum's out, you break in**

> **He uses the imperative verb at the beginning of the instruction, so it is clearly an order.**

He has been witness to the entire relaying of the story by Mark and Jan, but has kept quiet up until this point. This suggests that he was listening and considering the best course of action for the group. After the story has been relayed (page 23), stage directions state:

> *Pause. They all stare at LEAH and PHIL.*

> **This suggests that the others look to him for leadership in this crisis.**

Certainly, Leah always defers to him, whenever a decision has to be taken about a course of action.

Act 2, Scene 3 (pages 33-34, 40)

When, in the wood, Lou and Danny have explained that they have found the man, Leah turns to Phil who up to now in this scene has been silent:

LEAH: ...Phil? Any... any thoughts? Any words, any comments, any... ideas, any, any, any...thing? At all?

Later in the same scene (page 40), Leah turns to Phil again:

LEAH: Phil?

No answer.

Phil?

Pause. PHIL walks over to BRIAN and lays a hand on his shoulder.

PHIL: This is a bad situation. We didn't want this situation. But we've got this situation. It wasn't supposed to be like this. But it is like this.

Beat.

You're going in.

> **In his speeches, Phil is very clinical, direct and verbally economical, which creates a tense atmosphere, because others seem to focus on him and anticipate his actions with some uncertainty.**

No one really confronts him. They accept his direction, albeit reluctantly (**Act 1**, **Scene 3**, page 25):

DANNY: Is he taking the piss?

Danny may be reluctant to do as Phil says but he is still compliant and does not confront Phil directly. Nor do any of the others.

> **By the end of this scene in the wood (page 26) Phil asks: 'Any questions?' This is the first time he asks a question himself, but he is confident that he will not be challenged. And he is not:**

> *They stare at him open mouthed.*

> *He bends down. Picks up his Coke.*

> *Starts to drink his Coke.*

> **There is no evidence that anyone questions him.**

Act 3, Scene 3 (pages 57-58), Scene 4 (page 61)

A key quote that justifies his actions can be found in Act 3, Scene 3 (page 58):

> **PHIL: I'm in charge. Everyone is happier. What's more important; one person or everyone?**

> **This possibly reflects Kelly's key question which runs through the play, 'How far will we go to save the group?'**

> **Phil's body language is both reassuring and controlling. When addressing Lou in the same scene (page 57), the stage directions state that he:**

> *Places a hand on her shoulder, smiles, warm, reassuring.*

> PHIL: Everything is going to be fine.

In Act 3, Scene 4, their final connection in the play, when Phil silently offers Leah a sweet (page 61), ironically marks the first time he has shown her any affection or acknowledgement.

Act 4, Scene 2 (page 63)

◆ **In the final scene of the play, Act 4, Scene 2, Phil is sitting with Richard in the field, with Richard effectively taking over Leah's role. The stage directions (page 63) clearly state: *'PHIL is not eating.'* This is significant – something is wrong or missing from his existence. Does he realize he needs Leah? Or does he feel he has failed to hold the group together?**

John Tate

Act 1, Scene 3 (pages 12-13, 15-16)

We only encounter John Tate in one scene, Act 1, Scene 3, set in the woods. He attempts to lead by using fear to control others. But this approach fails as during the scene, he panics and is unable to control the others or the situation they have found themselves in.

He tries to ban the word 'dead' (page 15) and threatens to 'bite their face. Or something' if anyone uses the word again. The use of 'or something' indicates that, unlike Phil, he lacks clarity or direction and is out of his depth as a possible leader for this group.

■ **This is evident in his language. He repeats himself which shows his uncertainty:**

JOHN TATE: No, no, it's not, no, Lou, we're not

LOU: We are screwed.

JOHN TATE: No, Lou, we're not...it's not...we're not...nothing's....

LOU: It is.

When other characters challenge him, he backs down:

JOHN TATE: Everything is, everything's fine.

LOU: Fine?

JOHN TATE: Not fine, no

DANNY: Fine?

JOHN TATE: not fine exactly,...

The challenge to his leadership by Richard causes him further insecurity and he resorts to leading through fear, which he employs by threatening Lou, Danny and Richard.

> **His words are very patronizing as he talks down to each character:**

JOHN TATE: Danny, then you're on your own side, which is very, well, to be honest, very silly and dangerous.

Soon after, he refers to Brian as 'You crying piece of filth', and walks towards him, we assume, to continue his verbal intimidation of him. However the stage directions indicate: *'JOHN TATE stops'*, as Phil has entered the scene (page 19). Phil's arrival has a big impact on John Tate's behaviour. Later in the scene (page 23), after the story of Adam has been shared, John Tate poses the question: 'So, what do we do?'

Pause. They all stare at LEAH and PHIL.

It is evident that they do not see John Tate as a credible leader, but Phil. In contrast to Phil's use of language, John Tate uses interrogative sentence types (page 16):

> JOHN TATE: Ever since I came to this school haven't I been trying to keep everyone together? Aren't things better? For us? I mean not for them, not out there, but for us?

His speeches also focus on the first-person pronoun, himself, his feelings, and the need for him to be listened to and obeyed, rather than focusing on helping the situation. Again, his wish to ban the word 'dead' (page 15) highlights this:

...now I really am getting a little bit cross, do not use that word.

It is reported by Richard at the end of the play (**Act 4**, **Scene 2**, page 64) that John Tate 'found god':

'Yeah, Yeah. I know. He's joined the Jesus Army, he runs round the Shopping Centre singing and trying to give people leaflets.'

Danny

Act 1, Scene 3 (pages 14, 18)

Danny is the only character who seems to have an eye on his future, and on particular consequences which may affect him realizing his ambition. He has plans to further his education and become a dentist, but as in Act 1 Scene 3, he is continually concerned about the implications of the group's predicament on his intended goals (page 14):

DANNY: I can't get mixed up in this. I'm gonna be a dentist.

...

Dentists don't get mixed up in things. I've got a plan. I've got a plan John, I've made plans, and this is not...

However, he still allows John Tate to intimidate him into agreeing to be 'on his side' (page 18):

JOHN TATE: Are you on my side?

DANNY: Yes, I'm on your side!

Later in the same scene (page 25), Danny also complies with Phil's demands, and is still concerned about his own reputation (**Act 2**, **Scene 3**, page 35):

DANNY: This sort of stuff sticks, you know.

In the last scene of the play (**Act 4**, **Scene 2**, page 64), we learn from Richard that Danny has begun work experience at a dentist's:

RICHARD: He hates it. Can't stand the cavities, he says when they open their mouths sometimes it feels like you're going to fall in.

Act 2, Scene 3 (page 33)

Many of Danny's sentence types are declarative and he either makes observations or just supports what others have said with his own statements:

LEAH: Oh my god.

LOU: That's what we thought, we thought that, didn't we Danny.

DANNY: Yeah, we did.

LEAH: Are you sure? I mean are you...

DANNY: Definitely. He's in custody now. They're questioning him.

Danny provides a contrast to the others in the group as none of the others refer to their plans or the consequences of their actions on their lives or the lives of others. The character of Danny represents someone with a sense of morality; he is shocked by Phil's suggestion of taking Brian up to the grille, if he doesn't follow orders: 'Is he serious?' (Act 2, Scene 3, page 40). He is also alarmed that they are framing a man for something he didn't do: 'We can't let them think it's him' (Act 2, Scene 3, page 39). However, he has gone along with the plans and not really put up a strong enough resistance to the decisions made. He seems to be torn between loyalty to the group, his future career and the morality of what they are doing.

Richard

Act 1, Scene 3 (page 18)

Richard appears to be a second in command to Phil and he follows his leadership. At first he seems to be a strong character and someone who could succeed Phil as leader. Lou is scared of him, but although he stands up to John Tate: 'You shouldn't threaten me, John' (Act 1, Scene 3, page 17), he is eventually put in his place when John Tate turns the entire group against Richard by telling them to choose sides (page 18):

RICHARD: What do you mean by my side?

JOHN TATE: Have you got a side now, Richard?

RICHARD: No, no, there's no –

Act 2, Scene 3 (pages 36, 38)

Richard tends to put others down, and tends to be very negative in his responses to others. See these examples from Act 2, Scene 3, pages 38, 36:

CATHY: Richard, we showed initiative.

RICHARD: That is the most stupid –

...

CATHY: It was great.

RICHARD: It was shit.

> **He is also sarcastic towards other group members, as in this example, when Leah can't believe they have found a man that fits their fake description:**
>
> RICHARD: Why don't you pop down the station and say, 'excuse me, but the fat postman with the bad teeth doesn't actually exist, so why don't you let him go?'

By the last scene, Act 4 Scene 2, Richard – in place of Leah – sits in the field with Phil. His speech patterns are similar to Leah's. He seemingly talks about something unrelated to the group, attempts something physical to gain Phil's attention (walking on his hands), then brings his thoughts back to the current situation by discussing what has happened to the group.

Interestingly, he seems to have escaped any consequences unscathed.

Cathy

Act 2, Scene 3 (page 36)

From her entrance in Act 1, Scene 3 (page 15), Cathy is very excited by what has happened. On page 16 she claims that this is 'Better than ordinary life' and then says, 'I mean I'm not saying it's a good thing, but in a way it is'. She does not seem capable of empathizing with the victim or appreciating the seriousness of the event. She seems to support the leaders, initially John Tate who defends her by telling Danny, 'Don't tell Cathy to shut up' (page 17), and later she supports Phil's plans by taking the lead in agreeing to kill Adam. She seems to crave excitement. Later in the play, she focuses on the attention she might get from the TV cameras, but doesn't acknowledge the real reason they are there, and ignores Adam's plight:

CATHY: They might even give me money for it, do you think I should ask for money?

She appears not to acknowledge her actions in the group or show any remorse for what they have done to Adam.

It was in fact Cathy who obtained DNA evidence from an actual postman who fits the description Phil made up. Was this her way of impressing the leader and raising her status in the group? Was it a genuine mistake where she did not realize what she had done? Or was it to ensure that someone else would take the blame for the crime? (page 38):

CATHY: We showed...initiative, we –

LEAH: And who asked you to do that?

By the end of the play we learn that Cathy is now in charge and appears to have a sadistic nature. Phil has left the group so she assumes the role of leader she seems to have been craving.

Richard utters the final words on Cathy (Act 4, Scene 2, page 64):

RICHARD: Cathy doesn't care. She's too busy running things... She's insane. She cut off a first year's finger, that's what they say anyway.

Brian

Brian is seen by others in the group as the weakest link. Phil believes that Brian's vulnerability makes him the most plausible candidate to go to the police pretending that 'a man showed you his willy in the woods' (**Act 1**, **Scene 3**, page 24) and be believed. In a way Brian is a victim of his own 'honesty' and 'vulnerability' within a group who are now, for the most part, intent on lying to get themselves out of this situation.

He has a conscience and tries to resist lying. Initially, he suggests, 'I think we should tell someone' (page 19). He is the only one who wants to come clean. If they had followed his advice, the consequences may have been significantly different. He may be seen as weak, but he is the one who offers a solution he believes in, one which the other group members clearly do not support. He also resists Phil's instruction that he should go to the police, and give them a credible story: 'I'm not going in' (**Act 2**, **Scene 3**, page 39).

In many ways, he shows a greater ability to stand up to the group than Lou, who seems to accept everything that happens and offers no view. It's also noticeable how the other characters have categorized Brian along with Adam, in terms of status. For instance, Phil says, 'You'll fall into the cold. Into the dark. You'll land on Adam's corpse and you'll rot together' (**Act 2**, **Scene 3**, page 40).

When they discover Adam in the wood, Cathy says, 'I think his head's hurt' and Mark responds with 'Who, Brian or Adam's?' which implies that they see Brian as a victim, just as they saw Adam.

The first time we meet Brian in the play he enters with Richard and Cathy, crying. Is it possible that Brian's status is slightly higher than Adam's? After all it is Adam they attacked, not Brian. Possibly, the thought of what happened to Adam hangs over Brian like a cloud, and he offers some resistance to the group (page 39):

> 'I can't go in there, don't make me go in there, I'm not going in there'. This suggests that the group have the capacity to overrule him, and make him do what they want. This phrase is a syndetic, which suggests the panic felt by Brian at this point. The verb modality develops from 'can't' to 'not', which builds up and underlines Brian's insistence that he 'is not going'.

Brian is open and trusts that the matter will be resolved if we are honest. He dislikes lying, not simply due to the fear of being found out but because he seems to have a conscience (page 39): 'I'm crying because I'm lying and I feel terrible inside.'

> ✦ **Brian may well represent the voice of honesty, the resistance to lying, as well as Kelly's view that 'when we try to solve problems with a lie it doesn't work'. Brian represents the struggle we can experience by telling the truth, and wanting to be honest. When we lose faith in the value of telling the truth, we disconnect from reality and in Brian we witness a character that tries to be honest and is affected emotionally by the events of Adam's assumed death.**

He stands alone in a group which is less concerned with honesty than protecting themselves and their status within the group. We witness the consequences of Brian who has been forced to act against his conscience.

> ✦ **In this play, Kelly poses the question, 'How far will you go to save the group?' Outnumbered by the group and its demands, notably Phil's, what Brian thinks is the best course of action is outweighed. Had they taken Brian's original advice initially the group may have been saved from the consequences of their actions but, like Adam, Brian was victimized.**

He wasn't strong enough to insist on the course of action. The way he was perceived by the others and treated by them made it very difficult for his voice to be heard. John Tate referred to him as 'a crying little piece of filth' (Act 1, Scene 3, page 19) and when Richard is asked by Phil to take Brian to the head he says 'Me? But I hate him' so it is the power of the group which prevents Brian as an individual from listening to his conscience and acting upon it. He cannot deal with his guilt and is prescribed medication to help him cope. By Act 3, Scene 3 he is seen to revert to a childlike state of 'play' as his way of dealing with the events.

Lou

Lou is a follower of the group who does not want to draw attention to herself and avoids any kind of confrontation with the group. She is compliant with whoever is the leader at the time, and simply does as she is told. She is afraid of John Tate and possibly Richard, and her comments probably result in John Tate and Richard's confrontation (see Act 1, Scene 3, page 14).

> ▪ **Lou has no major speeches, which is probably why she seems to be less visible in the play. Instead she uses simple sentences or short phrases. Phrases such as 'We're screwed' (Act 2, Scene 3, page 34) make her appear naïve, less assertive, and reliant on being given instruction.**

She also seems to echo what others in the group have already mentioned, as if she is dependent on their influence and point of view. For instance (page 39):

BRIAN: I'm not going in.

RICHARD: You dick, Mark.

MARK: It was her idea!

LOU: Mark, you dick.

She also appears to believe the lies the group have created (page 35):

LOU: Because he saw him in the woods.

LEAH: He didn't

LOU: He did, he –

She is cut off by Leah.

Lou does not seem capable of keeping up with the lie the group have created, and it is not surprising that she becomes dominated by others.

Act 4, Scene 2 (page 64)

In Richard's commentary to Phil in the final scene on what the members of the group are now up to, we find out that Lou is best friends with Cathy:

RICHARD: Dangerous game. I feel sorry for her.

Adam

Act 1, Scene 3 (page 20)

Adam is the victim who has paid the ultimate price for remaining part of the gang. We hear from Jan and Mark his desire to be part of the group:

MARK: ...so we were sort of, well, alright, taking the piss, sort of. You know what he's like he was, sort of hanging around

JAN: Trying to be part of

MARK: Yeah, trying to be part of, yeah, yeah...

Adam would do anything to be part of the group. We hear about his horrific fate through Jan and Mark, who are trying to play down the seriousness of what they have done, convincing themselves that Adam was laughing about the things being done to him.

When Adam actually appears in Act 3, Scene 3 (page 49) we find out he has been living in a hedge. He has suffered a head injury, his memory is weak, and his speech is confused (Act 3, Scene 3, page 53).

 His monologue is vital to the atmosphere of the play and the terrifying world of the teenagers. Kelly shows the contrast between dark and light, symbolizing the delicate balance between life and death.

This page intentionally left blank

4

Introduction to the Use of Dimension Charts

**DIMENSION
CHARTS**

You will find an example of a completed Dimension Chart on the character of Leah. Creating a dimension chart is a useful starting point for you to explore characters. It is a way of examining different dimensions of a person.

Start by writing what you think you know about a particular character. I have provided some key quotes for you to consider, which tell you something about them, and also some writing prompts. Remember, you can infer things from what has been left unsaid, or where sentences are cut off in mid-stream.

Try some of the ones which are partly filled in and have a go at providing your views. Why not try two dimension charts on the same character. In the appendix, we have included some blank dimension charts, which you may wish to use in order to present a different view of the characters you have considered. You might like to try one for Leah and arrive at an alternative view of Leah, rather than the one provided here. Consequently you will need to locate quotes or stage directions or character interaction to support a possible alternative view of them. This might be a useful task to do with a friend, where you each create a dimension chart of the same character, interpreted differently.

How will these tasks help you prepare for your examination?

These tasks will help create your own personal response to characters, familiarize yourself with key quotes, and encourage you to consider alternative views on the same character, for when you come to writing a character essay for the examination. Remember, for a higher grade, it is important to provide a balanced argument and show awareness of different perspectives on the same character, before arriving at your own conclusion, based on textual evidence.

Exploring motivation levels of character

This task will help you to get inside the mind of a character, and put yourself in their shoes. It will engage you in thinking at a deeper level and answer questions in your head like 'What makes this character behave the way he/she does?' and 'Who has influenced him/her?'

COMPLETED DIMENSION CHARTS

You can complete blank dimension charts on one or more of the characters. I have provided a completed chart on Leah as an example, and you will be supported in completing step 3, the inference section of your dimension chart by studying appropriate parts of the play and by referring to the ideas in the Character Overview Section on pages 15 to 30.

How will these tasks help you to prepare for your examination?

Dimension charts, as the name suggests, give you an opportunity to connect all the dimensions of the play you will require for the examination. They help you to see the play as a whole and how elements are linked – for example the way characters reflect themes – and themes are reflected in characters. Your examination questions tend to focus on questions based on either Character or Theme, so the dimension charts are very useful preparation for that.

An example of a response to an examination question, based on the use of a dimension chart

The essay included in this section was created, as part of a revision practice, from the completed dimension chart, to illustrate how completing a dimension chart can really guide you in responding to an examination question.

Dimension Chart – Leah

Step 1
Initial Observations

Step 2
Textual Evidence

Step 3
Inferences we can make from textual evidence

What I think I know about Leah

Inferences

Leah is...
intelligent and imaginative.

She often...
goes off into 'flights of fancy' about her ideas related to other worlds.

She demonstrates...
perseverance and loyalty – she has known Phil since childhood and looks up to his leadership.

She is one of the few characters...
to demonstrate empathy.

She is concerned about...
the individuals in the group. She tries to solve the group's problems but ultimately turns to Phil to deal with it. She realizes at the end that being with Phil compromises her morality.

'What, like I talk too much? Is that it?' (**page 11**)

'Phil?' [No answer] 'Phil?' (**page 40**)

'It's Adam, Phil, Adam! We used to go to his birthday parties' (**page 58**)

'Empathy. That's what bonobos have. Amazing really, I mean they're exactly like chimps, but the tiniest change in their DNA...' (page 26)

Leah is a moral character and tries to reason with Phil (**page 58**).

She is sensible and able to think for herself and speak her mind.

She seems to fill the gaps provided by Phil's silences and gets frustrated by the lack of response.

She is concerned about Adam, and shows empathy for him so unlike Phil is not committed to sacrificing the individual to protect the group.

Leah likes to think and is interested in other worlds outside their immediate one (**page 26**).

She may be thinking about the group as chimps, and wishing they were more caring like bonobos.

She tends to look to Phil for leadership.

Dimension Chart – Cathy

Step 1
Initial Observations

Step 2
Textual Evidence

Step 3
Inferences we can make from evidence

What I think I know about Cathy

Inferences

Cathy is...

She often...

She demonstrates...

'I mean I'm not saying it's a good thing, but in a way it is' (**page 16**)

'they might even give me money for it, do you think I should ask for money?' (**page 36**)

JOHN TATE: Don't tell Cathy to shut up... (**page 17**)

She is one of the few characters...

She seems to have the ability to...

She is concerned about...

RICHARD: Cathy doesn't care. She's too busy running things... She's insane. She cut off a first year's finger, that's what they say anyway. (page 64)

Dimension Chart – Brian

Step 1
Initial Observations

Step 2
Textual Evidence

Step 3
Inferences we can make from evidence

What I think I know about Brian

Inferences

Brian is...

He often...

He is one of the few characters...

He seems to have the ability to...

He is concerned about...

'I think we should tell someone' (**page 19**)

'I'm not going in' (**page 39**)

PHIL: You'll fall into the cold. Into the dark. You'll land on Adam's corpse and you'll rot together. (**page 40**)

ADAM: 'I can't go in there, don't make me go in there, I'm not going in there' (page 39)

'...I'm crying because I'm lying and I feel terrible inside' (page 39)

RICHARD: Me? But I hate him! (page 24)

Dimension Chart – Danny

Step 1	Step 2	Step 3
Initial Observations	Textual Evidence	Inferences we can make from evidence

What I think I know about Danny		Inferences

Danny is...

He often...

He

'I can't get mixed up in this. I'm gonna be a dentist' (**page 14**)

'This sort of stuff sticks, you know' (**page 35**)

'We can't let them think it's him' (**page 39**)

'Dentists don't get mixed up in things. I've got a plan. I've got a plan John, I've made plans, and this is not...' (page 14)

He is one of the few characters...

He seems to have the ability to...

He is concerned about...

Dimension Chart – John Tate

Step 1
Initial Observations

Step 2
Textual Evidence

Step 3
Inferences we can make from evidence

What I think I know about John Tate

Inferences

John Tate is...

He often...

He demonstrates...

[To Danny]: ...You're on your own side, which is, well, to be honest, very silly and dangerous (**page 18**)

[To Brian]: You crying little piece of filth (**page 19**)

JOHN TATE: Everything is, everything's fine.

LOU: Fine? (**page 13**)

He is one of the few characters...

He seems to have the ability to...

He is concerned about...

'Ever since I came to this school haven't I been trying to keep everyone together? Aren't things better? For us? I mean not for them, not out there, but for us?' (**page 16**)

Dimension Chart – Phil

Step 1
Initial Observations

Step 2
Textual Evidence

Step 3
Inferences we can make from evidence

What I think I know about Phil

Inferences

Phil is...

He often...

He demonstrates...

He is one of the few characters...

He seems to have the ability to...

He is concerned about...

'Cathy, Danny, Mark, you go to Adam's house, you wait until his mum's out, you break in'
(**page 24**)

'Any questions?'

[They stare at him open mouthed.

He bends down.

Picks up his Coke.

Starts to drink his Coke.] **(page 26)**

Dimension Chart – Jan

Step 1	Step 2	Step 3
Initial Observations	Textual Evidence	Inferences we can make from evidence

What I think I know about Jan		Inferences

Jan is...

She often...

She demonstrates...

JAN: Dead?

MARK: Yeah

JAN: What, dead?

MARK: Yeah

(**page 9**)

She is one of the few characters...

She seems to have the ability to...

She is concerned about...

MARK: ...we can make him do –

JAN: That's when I went home

MARK: anything, yeah, only because you had to.

JAN: I wasn't there when –

(**page 22**)

Dimension Chart – Mark

Step 1
Initial Observations

Step 2
Textual Evidence

Step 3
Inferences we can make from evidence

What I think I know about Mark

Inferences

Mark is...

He often...

He demonstrates...

He is one of the few characters...

He seems to have the ability to...

He is concerned about...

MARK: Yes.

JAN: No, no

MARK: yes

JAN: no. No way, that's

MARK: I know

(page 44)

'I mean we were just having a laugh, weren't we, we were all, you know...'
(page 22)

JAN: I wasn't there when –

MARK: Only because you had to, you would've been there otherwise, you did all the...

Beat. **(page 22)**

Dimension Chart – Richard

Step 1
Initial Observations

Step 2
Textual Evidence

Step 3
Inferences we can make from evidence

What I think I know about Richard

Inferences

Richard is...

He often...

He demonstrates...

RICHARD: What do you mean by my side?

JOHN TATE: Have you got a side now, Richard?

RICHARD: No, no, there's no – (**page 18**)

CATHY: It was great.

RICHARD: It was shit.

(**pages 38-39**)

He is one of the few characters...

He seems to have the ability to...

He is concerned about...

RICHARD: Why don't you pop down the station and say, 'excuse me, but the fat postman with the bad teeth doesn't actually exist, so why don't you let him go?'

(**page 36**)

Dimension Chart – Adam

Step 1	Step 2	Step 3
Initial Observations	Textual Evidence	Inferences we can make from evidence

What I think I know about Adam

Inferences

Adam is...

He often...

He demonstrates...

He is one of the few characters...

He seems to have the ability to...

He is concerned about...

Mark: ...so we were sort of, well, alright, taking the piss, sort of. You know what he's like he was, sort of hanging around

Jan: Trying to be part of (**page 20**)

I was in a dark... Walking, crawling in this dark, when you're moving but with you hands and knees, crawl, crawling in this dark place and I don't remember things

(**page 53**)

5

Review of Plot and Character

Here is an opportunity to check your familiarity with the sequence of events in the play, *DNA*, as a storyboard:

We have provided the photographs of students your age trying out scenes physically from different moments in the play. The students who dramatised the episodes from the play, as seen in the photographs, often doubled up on characters, so you may not find all the characters in that particular episode in the actual photograph. More than one student often played the same role, so you will find the character of Phil depicted by two different students. You will also find that Cathy is depicted by two different students. However, the important thing is to examine the action and attitudes of the characters depicted by them so you can come to your own interpretations from the photographs shared here.

Task 1

Of course you may interpret the scenes differently at these moments and you can annotate the photographs with your own ideas. We think the images will help you visualize the sequence and the characters.

Task 2

Each photograph provided is accompanied by a quote and location.

See if you can order them in sequence.

● AO1:

Read, understand and respond to texts.

Students should be able to:

- Maintain a critical style and develop an informed personal response
- Use textual references, including quotations, to support and illustrate interpretations

SEQUENCING EVENTS ON A STORYBOARD

Jan and Mark

Act 1, **Scene 1** (page 10)

Location: A Street

MARK: Dead.

JAN: Oh.

MARK: Yes.

JAN: God.

MARK: Yes.

JAN: God.

MARK: Exactly.

Pause.

JAN: What are we going to do?

Leah and Phil

Act 1, **Scene 1** (page 10)

Location: A Field

LEAH: What are you thinking?

No answer.

No, don't tell me, sorry, that's a stupid, that's such a stupid –

You can tell me, you know. You can talk to me.

Jan and Mark

Act 1, **Scene 3** (page 22)

Location: A Wood

JAN: I mean he was still joking all the way, but

MARK: you could tell

JAN: He weren't really

MARK: fear

JAN: well

Danny, Richard, Cathy, Brian, Leah, Phil, Mark and Jan

Act 1, **Scene 3** (page 24)

Location: A Wood

PHIL: Cathy, Danny, Mark, you go to Adam's house, you wait until his mum's out, you break in

Jan and Mark

Act 2, **Scene 1** (page 30)

Location: A Street

JAN: That's what he said?

MARK: That's what he said, I'm saying that's what he said.

JAN: Shit.

MARK: Exactly.

Beat.

JAN: What are we going to do?

Phil and Leah

Act 2, **Scene 2** (page 32)

Location: A Field

LEAH: What have we done, Phil?

Danny, Lou and Phil

Act 2, **Scene 3** (page 34)

Location: A Wood

DANNY: What are we gonna do?

LOU: We're screwed.

Cathy

Act 2, **Scene 3** (page 38)

Location: A Wood

CATHY: Well, we thought, you know, I mean you'd given a description so we thought, well, I thought, you know, show initiative, we'll look for a fat balding postman with bad teeth.

Brian, Jan and Mark

Act 2, **Scene 3** (page 39)

Location: A Wood

BRIAN: I'm not going to the police station.

JAN: He has to. They're looking for him.

Phil, Leah, Lou, Danny, Richard, Jan, Mark and Brian

Act 2, **Scene 3** (page 39)

Location: A Wood

BRIAN: I can't go in. It was bad enough talking to them before, saying what I said, but I can't do it again.

Jan: They're searching everywhere for him. They want him to identify the man

Phil, Leah, Lou, Danny, Richard, Jan, Mark and Brian

Act 2, **Scene 3** (page 39)

Location: A Wood

BRIAN: I can't face it. They look at me. They look at me like I'm lying and it makes me cry. I can't stand the way they look at me. And then, because I cry, they think I'm telling the truth, but I'm crying because I'm lying and I feel terrible inside.

LOU: We're going to have to tell them.

LEAH: Maybe we could do something?

DANNY: We can' t do nothing, they want Brian

Cathy, Brian, Leah, Mark, Phil, Lou, Adam and Jan

Act 3, **Scene 3** (page 52)

Location: A Wood

JAN: What are we gonna do?

Cathy, Brian, Leah, Mark, Phil, Lou, Adam and Jan

Act 3, **Scene 3** (page 52)

Location: A Wood

LEAH: Phil?

What are we gonna...?

Phil?

Phil?

Say something Phil!

Pause. But PHIL says nothing.

Cathy, Brian, Leah, Mark, Phil, Lou, Adam and Jan

Act 3, **Scene 3** (page 52)

Location: A Wood

LEAH: What happened.

ADAM doesn't answer.

LEAH goes to him.

What happened?

6
Writer's Methods

Dennis Kelly says that 'language is very incomplete' as the characters talk 'like chimps picking fleas off each other'. On their own, the words very rarely give us full information. If language is incomplete in isolation, then we may also need to focus on the things unsaid or almost said, those things which are implied by the words or gaps between words, and of course the stage directions. In addition, we can work things out from how the characters speak and use language.

This guide includes reference to language, images and symbols throughout, so it is useful to cross-reference ideas and questions raised here, with those sections as appropriate, to help you understand how language fits into the concept of the play as a whole, including characters, themes and theatrical devices employed by Kelly.

IMAGES AND SYMBOLS

There are recurring images or symbols throughout the play: in addition to eating there are also the motifs of earth and dirt which remind us of the grave but also link to the 'feral' nature of the gang. Teeth too are mentioned which connects with the theme of consumption. There are strong images of light and dark throughout the play which may remind us of the contrast between good and evil. Consider Adam's description of his rebirth, the black pit into which Adam is thrown and the darkness Danny sees in the mouths of his patients. Light is emphasized by Leah in her descriptions of the sky and the sunsets; her reflections on the universe which are later echoed by Richard.

Think about why these images of 'good and evil' and 'light and dark' are employed by Kelly. How do they add to your understanding of the **themes** in the play? Why not look again at the section on **Themes** and see how these images support the themes?

You may also like to consider the symbols Kelly employs in the play, for example:

- Why does Leah refer often to the cosmos and the weather?

- What are the bonobos and chimps symbolic of? Do they tell us something about the nature of a gang or group?

- What might Adam be a symbol of? Is that symbol intended as a biblical reference?

- What about the symbols of teeth and food, food which Phil is constantly preparing and eating throughout his meetings with Leah in the field? What do they symbolize?

- What do the **settings** of the woods, the field and the street symbolize?
  (See the section on **Settings** for some ideas on this.)

- Why might Kelly refer to 'earth' and 'dirt' a lot throughout the play?

- How does Kelly use images of light and dark in the play? What is their significance in our understanding of the play and its **themes**? (See the section on **Theatrical elements** and the use of **tension** for some ideas on this, as well as the section on **Themes**.)

USE OF LANGUAGE BY CHARACTERS

Characters often have different sentence types:

The main sentence type is **declarative**, which is a statement.

Another sentence type is **interrogative**, which is simply a question with a question mark at the end.

A sentence type known as **exclamatory** simply means it has an exclamation mark on the end of it.

Finally, an **imperative** sentence type: a commanding verb at the start of the sentence such as 'Cut' or 'Slice', as used in recipes. If someone is giving an order they use an imperative verb at the start. Phil's character provides examples of this: see page 24 where he orders his peers to 'go to Adam's house, you wait, you break in'.

The use of language by the characters also contributes to **the structure**, as sentence structure is a **structural device**. **Structure** also has an effect on time, as there is a need to pace the text. At the start of the play, Jan and Mark establish a fast-moving 'zingy' pace, by way of monosyllabic devices such as 'Dead?', 'Yeah', 'What, dead?', 'Yeah'. In contrast, Scene 2 presents a more reflective monologue from Leah. In her scenes, Leah uses rhetorical questions such as, 'They murder each other, did you know that?'

Monologues, too, are a **structural device,** because they allow us to focus on one character. The use of the monologue also **creates tension**, because it gives us this shift in perspective and this shift in focus creates tension. The monologue on page 26 begins with an adverb, 'Apparently', and develops into a hypothesis from Leah that 'bonobos are our nearest relatives' and she next uses a connective to put forward a contrasting view – 'but they're not, they are completely different'. She uses comparative language – 'whereas' – so she looks at both sides, and tries to be tentative in her conclusions. She possibly creates, by implication, a social parallel to the group of young people in the play: 'They kill and sometimes torture each other to find a better position within the social structure.' Is this Kelly's way of anticipating what is going to happen to the group? Does it give us some indication that Phil will be replaced as a leader by Cathy and that together they will kill Adam?

We see the use of ellipses in this monologue, when she says, 'but the tiniest change in their DNA...' and she uses emotive language, like 'hounded', 'torture' and 'feeling pain', whilst posing rhetorical questions: 'How do you do it?' and 'What would you do?' Rhetorical questions encourage us to think and reflect.

You will find examples of the use of language by particular characters under the section **Overview of Characters**.

Kelly may have employed particular linguistic features, as the play is intentionally written for young people. Of course, this may result in constraints of dramatic impact, as the characters will be performed by a group of young people. There are very few expletives; 'piss' and 'shit' are the ones used most often – perhaps linking with the motifs of earth and dirt that run throughout the play. Dennis Kelly might be excused for using more – after all the play involves a group of street-wise and perhaps hardened teenagers involved in a terrible crime. However, by using fewer swear words, the play can be deemed appropriate for older teenagers without restricting it to 18 plus.

(This is also relevant to **CONTEXT**, and you may refer to this when discussing context in your examination answer.)

In *DNA*, Kelly's characters use colloquial and informal language, the dialogue being the kind we might associate with a group of young people who are anxious and panicked by the potential consequences of their actions. Kelly attempts to replicate the rhythms of authentic speech patterns including hesitations, reluctant starters, and unfinished utterances. There are several examples of this in Leah's long speeches, such as in Act 1, Scene 2 (page 10): 'that's such a stupid –' and 'I won't, I won't...'. Here Kelly has employed the use of an elliptical pause, followed by an ellipsis. The hyphen in the elliptical pause is used quite a lot throughout the play, where unrelated ideas are commented on. The elliptical pause (three dots) shows something is missing and we draw our own conclusions which may lead to inference.

So, what is in Leah's mind at that point? What is the missing thought here?

During Phil's interaction with others in Act 1, Scene 3 (pages 25-26), his language is very instructional. He uses the second person pronoun a lot – 'Lou, Danny and Jan **you take** the shoes' – as well as the imperative verb '**take**', which supports this instructional style. As he develops his instructions to the group, his language shifts to the third person pronoun: 'John Tate comes forward and says **he** thinks he saw Adam...'. There is a difference here; he is now including the group members, and passing on responsibility to them to carry out the action. This may be a persuasive device, and it marks a change; he appears to use the third person pronoun when he persuades them that they won't take the blame. It is more general and shifts where the blame will lie, and this is supported by his conclusion where he includes the inclusive '**we**': '...if everyone keeps their mouth shut **we** should be fine'.

Phil rarely asks questions, although at the end of this scene asks, 'Any questions?', after he has dictated the details of what each of them must do. At this stage, I suggest, he is very confident that he will be asked no questions.

In John Tate's language, Kelly makes use of the syndetic 'and', and along with lots of conjunctions contributes to his rambling speeches, which lack clarity. He finishes Lou's sentence; where she says, 'Tricky?', he interrupts with 'Situation'. His sentences are mainly interrogative and, unlike Phil, he asks a lot of questions.

In Act 4, Scene 2 (page 65), Richard uses descriptive language, referring to the 'big wind of fluff'. With 'big', he uses an intensifying but very basic adjective and he adds a simple noun phrase in 'wind of fluff'. In using the imperative verb, 'Imagine', he invites the audience in. Via repetition and simple similes, he evokes a childlike view of the world: 'I was an alien in a cloud'.

THEATRICAL DEVICES, INCLUDING USE OF TENSION

Tension, an element of surprise, is built in to the structure of the play, for example, the revelation that a man has been framed for their 'crime' and the discovery that Adam is still alive. Examine these moments in the text and consider their impact on the audience.

Dramatic tension created between and amongst characters also occurs when the writer has built these devices into the action/dialogue/sequence of events they experience as characters within the play.

Tension levels – different kinds of tension and their impact

Tension is the development of suspense in a performance. As the audience anticipates certain outcomes in the plot, the tension builds. I have found Dorothy Heathcote's tension levels useful when working with young people engaged in drama, and also useful when examining plays. You can find Heathcote's tension levels if you go on to www.mantleoftheexpert.com.

I have located examples of five of these tension levels within Kelly's writing and I am sure you may find more, but see if any of these make sense to you.

Lou and John Tate

Act 1, Scene 3 (A Wood, page 14)

LOU: He's dead, John.

JOHN TATE: Alright, I'm not denying it, am I denying? No, I'm

LOU: He's dead.

JOHN TATE: Well, don't keep saying it.

This tension is created by the 'uncontrollable presence which threatens' (level 1). The presence of Adam's 'death' creates tension here, as John Tate seems to be in denial about the reality of the situation they find themselves in, while the presence of 'death' is something beyond their control and which threatens the entire group with potentially damaging consequences. Lou's repetition of the word 'dead' reminds us of this uncontrollable threat.

Cathy, Leah, Richard Danny and Lou

Act 2, Scene 3 (A Wood, page 38)

Notice a different kind of tension created in the following dialogue:

CATHY: We showed...initiative, we –

LEAH: And who asked you to do that?

CATHY: Richard, we showed initiative.

RICHARD: That is the most stupid –

DANNY: Oh, Jesus.

CATHY: Why?

LEAH: Why? Because there is now a man in prison who is linked to a non-existent crime, answering a description that Brian gave.

LOU: Oh, Jesus Christ.

CATHY: But isn't that...

LEAH: No, Cathy, it is not what we wanted.

This tension is created by a breakdown in communication and also created by the threat from stupidity and foolish carelessness. Cathy has clearly not thought through the implications of her action, and has foolishly not fully realized or cared sufficiently about the possible consequences for an innocent man.

DNA by Dennis Kelly: Routes to Revision

Brian and Jan

Act 2, Scene 3 (A Wood, page 39)

In the following extract, the character of Brian demonstrates a different kind of tension:

BRIAN: I'm not going to the police station.

JAN: He has to. They're looking for him.

BRIAN: I can't go in. It was bad enough talking to them before, saying what I said, but I can't do it again.

JAN: They're searching everywhere for him. They want him to identify the man.

BRIAN: I can't identify him, I can't go in there, don't make me go in there, I'm not going in there.

Here, the tension is created by a breakdown in relationships and differences within the group, with Brian insisting he can't go back to the police station. Others can see that this action is vital in saving them from the consequences.

Leah and Phil

Act 3, Scene 4 (A Wood, page 60)

In the following extract, Leah tries to stop Phil and Cathy killing Adam:

LEAH: No, Cathy, don't, stop, Cathy...?

But she goes, taking BRIAN with her. LEAH turns to PHIL.

Phil?

Phil?

Please!

Please, Phil!

But PHIL just walks away.

The tension is created here by the 'loss of faith in companions'. At this point Leah sees the hopelessness of trying to dissuade Phil and Cathy from their intentions.

56

Jan and Mark

Act 3, Scene 1 (A Street, page 45)

Here Jan and Mark relay the new information that Adam has been found alive in the woods:

MARK: In the woods, Cathy found him in the woods

JAN: Cathy?

MARK: Yes.

JAN: Cathy found him...?

MARK: Yes, she

JAN: in the woods?

MARK: Yes.

Beat.

This extract creates tension because of dangers known in advance. They now face the danger of confronting the results of their crime. The setting of the woods has now taken a more sinister turn – it feels like a forbidden place or at least one where the 'cover up' for their crime will be revealed through Adam. This creates anticipation for the audience who wonder what the group's next steps will be.

● AO2:

Analyze the language, form and structure used by a writer to create meanings and effects, using relevant subject terminology where appropriate.

How theatre elements, including choice of settings, build the atmosphere of the play for an audience

In this section you will consider how ideas are related to the concept of a play in performance, and how those responses can help you address AO3, (Context); a play to be performed and in this case, by young people and specifically for young people. Context is evident here as we examine Kelly's theatrical devices applied to a play in performance (genre), by considering his designed settings.

The following tasks will also meet some of the requirements of structural devices (AO2) as we examine how Kelly constructs settings to contribute to the play's meanings.

Settings

Consider the locations Kelly has decided on for each scene in his play *DNA*.

Are any locations more public and others more private?

- A Street
- A Field
- A Wood

What kind of moods and images do you associate with these locations?

What are the important moods and emotions in the scene?

Are there any words in the text that gives us a clue?

Make a list of these words:

The following words I found significant:

A Street:

'Dead?' / 'Yeah.' / 'What, dead?' / 'Yeah.'

(Conversational) A street suggests people, chatting, shopping, busy movement.

A Field:

'What are you thinking?'

(Reflective) A field suggests an escape or a romance, an open area where you can see if anyone approaches.

A Wood:

> 'Dead. He's dead.'
>
> (Dramatic)
>
> 'So what do we do?'
>
> (Plotting secretly) – suggests a hiding place, secret meetings. Brian says, 'D'you ever feel like the trees are watching you?' as if we go there to hide, to conceal things.

The key question, then, is: how does the writer, Kelly, convey these moods and emotions?

The basic elements of theatre are defined, thus:

DARKNESS	**LIGHT**
SOUND	**SILENCE**
STILLNESS	**MOVEMENT**

In the theatre, we use these contrasting elements to create atmosphere and if you try this task I think you will get a sense of the play as it is performed, beyond just being words on a page. They will help you appreciate the genre of the writing – a play designed to be put on its feet in the theatre, and deliberately aimed at young people.

Darkness and Light: This may be suggested by the mood changes (from dark to light), an actual change from day to night or speech which describes a dark mood contrasted with a light mood.

Sound and Silence: This could be obvious in an episode from the play, where sound is contrasted with silence, or it may be implied by the actions of people, or people leaving the scene where you imagine silence falls and that feels right. Phil and Leah's dialogue certainly uses the contrast between sound and silence (note the pauses here – what might they convey to an audience?). The sounds of the beat frequently punctuate the action.

Stillness and Movement: Movement followed by stillness may be obvious in some parts of the play and in other parts it may be suggested by the dialogue or stage directions, or by the location. These elements may be suggested by the mood, the pace of the dialogue or moments where a pause is suggested.

Here are some extracts which employ theatrical elements in this way:

Darkness and Light

The following extract clearly demonstrates the elements of **dark and light:**

Act 3, **Scene 4** (A Wood, page 53)

ADAM: I fell, I falled into, I fell onto this...

wake, woke, wake up. I woke up with liquid on my head, leaves, dead and rotting. I remember leaves, but just dark maybe a light high, high, high, high, high...

above and, I drank the liquid it was blood, there was, it was mine, so I, it's not wrong because it was my

...

And then I came out.

I saw this

light, this daylight light, I saw this light and went that way, towards, and I thought I died because that's what people

go to the light

Kelly has included images of darkness throughout the play. What do you make of these contrasting images? What do they mean? Are they a way of symbolizing the confused images in Adam's mind? Is light a symbol of life or death? There are references to 'hedges' and 'warrens' in this scene in the woods which create a dark atmosphere.

Sound and Silence

The following extract clearly demonstrates the elements of **sound and silence:**

Act 1, **Scene 2** (A Field, page 11)

LEAH: ...I talk too much, what a crime, what a sin, what an absolute catastrophe, stupid, evil, ridiculous, because you're not perfect actually, Phil. Okay? There. I've said it, you're not...

You're a bit...

You're...

Pause. She sits.

What is going on in that silence? What do you imagine Leah and Phil are doing at that moment and why?

Stillness and Movement

A noticeable shift between movement and stillness takes place in Act 2, Scene 3. When Brian, Richard, Leah, Mark, Lou, Danny and Jan are in a state of tension concerning Brian's refusal to go to the police station, there may be elements of agitated **movement:**

Act 2, Scene 3 (A Wood, page 39)

LOU: Mark, you dick.

BRIAN: I'm not going to the police station.

JAN: He has to. They're looking for him.

Then, on page 40, Phil enters, to take charge of the situation:

LEAH: Phil?

No answer.

Phil?

Pause. PHIL walks over to BRIAN and lays a hand on his shoulder.

PHIL: This is a bad situation. We didn't want this situation. But we've got this situation. It wasn't supposed to be like this. But it is like this.

Beat.

You're going in.

By now, there is a sense of stillness which contrasts starkly with the arguments amongst the group on the previous page. This continues on page 41:

PHIL: Richard'll take you. You take a look at that man and you say it's him. You say it's the man in the woods. That's what you do. Okay?

Slowly, BRIAN nods.

Everyone else stays calm. Keep your mouths shut. Tell no one or we'll all go to prison. Just get on with things.

He starts to eat his pie. They stare at him.

With the other characters now giving Phil their full attention, this is a very clear example of how the animation earlier in the scene has given way to stillness. What does this change of atmosphere in the play suggest? Does it emphasize Phil's power – that when he is present people focus on him, on his instructions and directions? Is this why Kelly has used this shift in atmosphere in this scene?

Why not look at some other scenes in *DNA* which interested you and see if you can notice how Kelly included these elements, either so that they are explicitly obvious – as in the example of Adam provided – or implied by the stage directions, as in the final example related to Phil's power over the group. What effects do such devices have?

● **AO1:**

Read, understand and respond to texts.

Students should be able to:

- Maintain a critical style and develop an informed personal response

- Use textual references, including quotations, to support and illustrate interpretation.

● **AO2:**

Analyze the language, form and structure used by a writer to create meanings and effects, using relevant subject terminology where appropriate.

● **AO3:**

Show understanding of the relationships between texts and the contexts in which they were written.

● **AO4:**

Use a range of vocabulary and sentence structure for clarity, purpose and effect, with accurate spelling and punctuation.

This page intentionally left blank

7

Themes

What is a Theme?

The Russian theatre director, Konstantin Stanilavski, talked about the 'ruling idea' in a play. He called this the 'super-objective' – the idea that inspired the dramatist to write the play in the first place.

You might decide that the 'ruling idea' of *DNA* is 'The group versus the individual' or 'Consequences of our actions' or 'Responsibilty', 'Gangs', or 'Good versus evil'.

When working with young people, Dorothy Heathcote often begins by asking, 'What is this play about?' If they can answer that question, she argues, 'It is like a mushroom cloud, spreading over the terrain of the play. They begin to see more and more connections.'

A theme is concerned with one or more ideas central to the play. It is more than simply what the play is about, i.e. the plot. It is about the ideas the play presents, or the questions it raises for you, the audience.

For example, if I ask you, 'What is *Cinderella* about?' you might respond with, 'It's about a girl who is treated cruelly, by her sister and stepmother, and ends up marrying a prince'. In other words you would give me a brief summary of the plot. But if I was to ask you, 'What is it really about?' I would be asking you to look beyond the plot, and beneath the surface of the story, the characters and their motivations. I would be asking you to think about the meanings of the play in a wider context than the play itself. I would be asking you to tell me about the themes suggested by the plot and characters and their actions.

In *Cinderella*, for example, we may find the following themes:

Bullying

Royalty

Hierarchy

Poverty

Magic

Parenting

Power

Change

Deceit

Manipulation

Social Status

Child Neglect

And I am sure you can think of others.

If I ask you what *DNA* is about you might say, 'It is a play about a group of teenagers who panic when they realize they have done something bad, seriously bad.'

But, if I ask you what the themes are, you might find the following themes in *DNA*:

Gangs

Consequences

Deceit

Responsibility

Friendship

Power

Leadership

Victims

Childhood/Adolescence

Violence

And of course, you will probably think of others.

> **KEY
> THEMES**

Gangs

One of the themes is the idea of a gang or a close-knit group, which we are presented with early in the play. Initially in disparate groups, the characters come together as one group, as the nature of the 'crime' is gradually revealed through the panic they experience in response to the death of Adam. Power struggles are evident within the group, as when John Tate attempts to exert his leadership and is challenged by Richard. Phil becomes the group's leader, taking a very clinical approach and devising a well-constructed plan.

The play's writer Dennis Kelly says:
'*DNA* is connected to a particular period of my adolescence when someone new came into my circle of friends at school *and we turned from human beings into this pack of animals*. There were these concentric rings of popularity. If you were at the centre, that was a good place to be, but you always knew you could be pushed to the outside. When you were on the outside, that was horrible. That's what *DNA* is about.'

Do some people do things that they never would have done alone because they are led by others? Are the morals of a group different to those of an individual?

The play raises Kelly's question of 'How far will we go to save the group?'

Bullying

As far as Kelly is concerned the play is not about bullying. According to him, the bullying has already happened before the start of the play, through the stoning of Adam, which suggests psychological bullying as well as physical abuse. Jan and Mark provide us with this information, and reflect on it. Meanwhile, is Phil guilty of using bullying tactics against his girlfriend Leah, through his lack of response? Are

John Tate's attempts at leadership a form of bullying? How do the others react to it? That might give you an indication: where there are bullies, there are usually victims.

The other members of the group are manipulated by Phil. Is that bullying? Or is Phil trying to help the group?

Responsibility

The play raises the question of responsibility. Kelly's question which drives the play is, 'How far will we go to save the group?' When asked why he wrote the play, he says, 'It was really what was in my head at the time about group responsibility and the individual.' He describes contexts which influenced him: 'The Iraq war and the July bombings in London. We were living in a climate of fear and we still are and it's getting worse. Whenever these sort of things happen, we think about civil liberties and the threat to them.'

While Jan and Mark seem to have been responsible for the alleged death of Adam, it is clear that the entire group take on the responsibility of what happened, guided by Phil's leadership. Jan and Mark sidestep the gravity of their actions with references to 'laughing' and being in 'stitches', recalling Adam's struggle to be part of the group (he ate leaves, stole vodka and had cigarettes stubbed out on him). Leah, as does Brian, seems to realize the human cost of the event they have become caught up in. Leah refers to Adam as someone they both knew as children and Brian is troubled by his conscience when lying to the police.

The gang share the 'burden' of responsibility, a device which ensures that they all keep quiet. When Phil states, 'I'm in charge. Everyone is happier. What's more important: one person or everyone?', he makes them all feel that they cannot step back from the solutions he puts forward. Finally, he decides that ending Adam's life is the only solution for the group. This means that they become responsible for a deliberate ending of a life, rather than an accidental one.

Childhood/Adolescence

Kelly deliberately wrote this play for young people, and exclusively presents their world in it. As he explains, 'I wrote this play as I wrote any play – I didn't water it down for young people as young people are bright and they are sharp. Kids like thinking and Leah is really profound when she mentions that when we first discovered chimps we didn't know about bonobos 'cos they looked the same.' He continues, 'In their world, it is different to the adult world – kids always had to solve their own problems, the world of childhood can be terrifying.' There are no adults and the only ones referred to are people who may jeopardize their plans, or those who can be convinced by their deceit, such as the police. Brian's suggestion, early on, that they should tell someone is ignored.

Friendship

What is meant by friendship? Is it meaningful in this context? Kelly suggests that performers can change names and even genders of characters – would this change the dynamics of the group?

If friendship includes a need for loyalty, then the gang members in *DNA* do demonstrate this group loyalty. Their actions surrounding the alleged death of Adam demand group loyalty. The first part of the play focuses entirely on the group's friendship – the outside world is not important. The reported sentimental outpouring of friendship and grief for the 'dead boy' contrasts with the group's collective and individual sense of responsibility and guilt. As a consequence, the friendships in the group start to fall apart. Leah gives up on her friendship with Phil, claiming he is not human. While she responds emotionally to the situation concerning Adam, Phil clinically tries to solve the problem for the group. The situation magnifies differences within the group and threatens the security of friendship. Leadership within the group also changes as when some leave, and Cathy replaces Phil as a leader. In the final act, Kelly has employed a structural device to signify the breakup of friendships. Unlike the 4 scenes in previous acts, there are now only 2 scenes. The Wood is now absent and we only visit the Field once, which signifies both the end of the group as a collective and the end of Leah and Phil's friendship.

Hierarchy

What Kelly told us:
'*DNA* is connected to a particular period of my adolescence when someone new came into my circle of friends at school *and we turned from human beings into this pack of animals*. There were these concentric rings of popularity. If you were at the centre, that was a good place to be, but you always knew you could be pushed to the outside. When you were on the outside, that was horrible. That's what *DNA* is about.'

Kelly suggests young people turn into animals; 'pack' suggests wolves, which suggests that together, as a pack, they can become dangerous. The person at the centre is the leader, but Kelly suggests that the role is ever changing as the circles of popularity shift.

John Tate's leadership early in the play is challenged by Richard, but he remains on the higher level of the hierarchy, up until Phil's entrance in Act 1. Notice the change in his response and status at this point. By the end of the play, we gather that Cathy has replaced Phil as leader.

See what changes you notice in hierarchy, throughout the play.

You may like to come up with new answers to the question 'What is the play really about?' (in other words, what the writer is saying and what the play makes you think about), where your thoughts shift from the play's situation and plot to its general themes.

For example:

Leadership

Growing up

The breakdown in civilisation

Here are some questions which get you thinking about themes in the play:

Are children innocent?	**How far are we responsible for other people?**

Is lying a way of solving a problem?

What do we mean by right and wrong?

Should we listen to our conscience or be guided by others?

Are we responsible for the consequences of our actions?

Are people born victims or do they become victims?

When is it right to challenge leadership?

8

Contexts

What was the idea, 'the ruling idea', which first inspired Dennis Kelly to write the play *DNA*?

In what context was the play written? Kelly describes what was in his head at the time he wrote the play:

'It was really what was in my head at the time about group responsibility and the individual, The Iraq War and the July bombings in London. The original play DNA was first published in 2008. We were all living in a climate of fear and we still are and it's getting worse. Whenever these sorts of things happen we think about civil liberties and the threat to them and the right to protect the good group. It's not about bullying – that has already happened before the play starts – it's more about consequences. When we try to solve problems with a lie it doesn't work. We went to war because Saddam Hussein is a bad man, but there are shades of grey in all of us as there are in people in the group in 'DNA'. I don't believe in good or bad. The question is: How far will we go to save the group?'

He continues:

'When I write a play I don't have an answer. I think about a question I don't have an answer to – there's never an easy answer as this makes it more interesting although the play does pose this moral question.'

I wonder: what questions does the play raise for you?

While writing *DNA*, Kelly might have been inspired by statements such as the following:

'We believe [Saddam] has, in fact, reconstituted nuclear weapons.'
US Vice President Dick Cheney on television's Meet the Press (16 March 2003)

The reporter Christopher Scheer responded on Alternet with:

'There was, and is, absolutely zero basis for this statement.'

Another possible example:

'We know where [Iraq's weapons of mass destruction] are. They're in the area around Tikrit and Baghdad and east, west, south and north somewhat'
US Secretary of Defense, Donald Rumsfeld, in statements to the press (30 March 2003)

According to Christopher Scheer, 'No such weapons were found.'

So the specifics of the play reflect the wider issues in the world where there are consequences for actions taken. If *DNA* examines the consequences of a group of young people covering up a lie, then the Iraq war may be seen as a consequence of a cover up for the actual motivations for the invasion of Iraq.

Was Saddam Hussein's execution an example of the sacrifice of an individual for the sake of a group? You might consider its effect on the country of Iraq and its people today.

See if you can think of other parallels with social or political events outside the play.

Can you think of other examples in the world where people have tried to solve problems by lying and the consequences have not been good for them?

Can you think of any examples in the world of how people have gone to great lengths to save the group?

Contexts also refer to the setting (location) in which the work is placed. For this, Kelly has located *DNA*, specifically designed for young people, in settings they can identify with: a street, a wood, a field. Kelly was commissioned to write this play for the National Theatre in 2008. It deliberately excludes adults so that we focus on the world from the perspectives of these young people and how they try to make sense of the predicament they have created. You will find more ideas related to settings in section 6, where they contribute to Kelly's theatrical devices.

● AO1:

Read, understand and respond to texts.

Students should be able to:

- Maintain a critical style and develop an informed personal response

- Use textual references, including quotations, to support and illustrate interpretation.

● AO2:

Analyze the structure used by a writer to create meanings and effects, using relevant subject terminology where appropriate.

● AO3:

Show understanding of the relationships between texts and the contexts in which they were written.

A Note about Contexts

AO3 is the understanding of the relationship between the ideas in the text and the contexts of the text. You can consider context in a flexible way. It may refer to:

- The time in which it was written

- The context in which the text is set: location, social structures and features, cultural contexts and periods of time

- Literary contexts such as genres, and also the contexts in which texts are engaged with by different audiences, taking the reader outside the text in order to inform understanding of the meanings being conveyed

- The acknowledgement of the universality of a literary text which is an integral part of relating to it contextually

This page intentionally left blank

9

Tackling the Question

In this section we offer you two extracts from the beginnings of essays on *DNA* in answer to examination questions. Take a look at them and see if you can differentiate them. See if you can identify the reasons why one been awarded higher marks than the other? We apply the examiner's assessment criteria to show how marks are awarded. Read through them and this will help you understand what the examiner is looking for when you are tackling the question.

Essay Title

In *DNA*, Phil says 'I'm in charge.' How does Kelly present Phil as a leader?

Leaders are in Positions of Power; sometimes they are placed in that position, and sometimes they emerge because there is a need for someone to rescue the group in an individual or wider collective context.

In the play, *DNA*, Dennis Kelly presents Phil as a character who demonstrates perspicacity in his use of leadership qualities. He appears to demonstrate a strategic approach to his role as leader.

The audience is first introduced to Phil when he demonstrates his authority over the group, by giving instructions to alleviate a crisis – namely the crisis related to the 'cover up' concerning the stoning of Adam.

'Cathy, Danny, Mark, you go to Adam's house, you wait until his mum's out, you break in.' He shows precision of thought, with an economy of language. It is syndetic in structure, showing a deliberate omission of unnecessary details which could cause confusion. His use of the second-person pronoun, 'you', three times in the same sentence, consolidates that precision. He omits any unnecessary conjunctions, in order to focus the other characters on the actions he wishes them to carry out.

Persuasive techniques are employed here by Kelly; second-person pronouns precede specific verbs: 'Go', 'Wait' and 'Break'. The effect of these verbs builds up the intensity, with the use of an ascending tricolon which enables the instructees to gauge the level of participation needed to carry out Phil's specific commands. He is judicious in his use of instructions for these specific characters, giving them graduated instructions, in logical, specific steps.

In this quotation, Phil's leadership qualities are clear from his precise use of language towards other characters. It demonstrates focus, clarity of thought and confidence in his group status: his authority is unchallenged and probative in approach.

Phil's unchallenged leadership position is further reinforced...

● AO1:

Read, understand and respond to texts.

Students should be able to:

- Maintain a critical style and develop an informed personal response

- Use textual references, including quotations, to support and illustrate interpretation.

● AO2:

Analyze the language, form and structure used by a writer to create meanings and effects, using relevant subject terminology where appropriate.

● AO3:

Show understanding of the relationships between texts and the contexts in which they were written.

● AO4:

Use a range of vocabulary and sentence structure for clarity, purpose and effect, with accurate spelling and punctuation.

● Assessment Comments

Candidate's response uses a judicious and analytical approach throughout the response.

Analyzes the effect of the writer's methods and language and analyzes the effects using specific technical vocabulary. Skilfully integrates contextual references to support analysis.

Notional Mark: 27

Notional Grade: 8

Notional Level: 6

Examiner's Tip: If this essay maintained this level of analysis throughout, including additional points demonstrating an alternative viewpoint regarding Phil, it is likely this would achieve the highest grade

In *DNA*, Phil says, 'I'm in charge'. How does Kelly present Phil as a leader?

Write about:

- How Kelly presents the character of Phil

- How Kelly uses the character of Phil to explore ideas about leadership

Kelly presents the character of Phil, in his play *DNA*, as a leader who employs a range of strategies, to lead the group. We witness Phil interacting with his peers in a contemporary play, specifically written for young people. Throughout, there are no adults present, so the problems they encounter have to be resolved within the group.

When the audience are first introduced to Phil, he is instructing his peers about what action to take; this is illustrated when he says: 'Cathy, Danny, Mark, you go to Adam's house, you wait until his mum is out, you break in.'

In this quotation, we see that the writer has employed three specific verbs, 'Go', 'Wait' and 'Break', to demonstrate what specific actions he requires from the other characters.

When Mark and Jan have relayed their story of the stoning of Adam, there is a pause and they all stare at Phil, which suggests that he is seen as the one who will make the final decisions.

Many times during the play, Leah asks 'Phil?', as addressing a leader. Even when characters show reluctance they still conform to what Phil requests or demands. For example, when Danny says 'Is he taking the piss?', he is not confronting Phil directly and does not challenge him.

Phil is constantly eating or drinking coke throughout the play particularly in the scenes in the field. These actions may be used by the character as a way of distracting from Leah's constant talking or a way of helping him think through the next steps of the plan for the group.

Kelly presents Phil as a leader who doesn't listen to others, or discuss anything. His word seems to be the only one that matters and all the others go along with it. In the final scene, Phil stops eating. This is significant, because Leah has left, and maybe he has also stopped thinking. Kelly has used a cyclical structure to show how circumstances change. We always see the same people in the same places, but they change each time we visit them. The final time we see Phil with Richard, he seems to have lost his drive for leadership, and though his position remains the same, circumstances have changed.

It is possible that Phil as a leader faces the consequences of being a very dictatorial leader, who has failed to consider the roles of others in making decisions and possibly neglected to understand the views of others. In doing so, he has lost sight of the human cost of the cover up.

● AO1:

Read, understand and respond to texts.

Students should be able to:

- Maintain a critical style and develop an informed personal response

- Use textual references, including quotations, to support and illustrate interpretation.

● AO2:

Analyze the language, form and structure used by a writer to create meanings and effects, using relevant subject terminology where appropriate.

● AO3:

Show understanding of the relationships between texts and the contexts in which they were written.

● AO4:

Use a range of vocabulary and sentence structure for clarity, purpose and effect, with accurate spelling and punctuation.

● Assessment Comments

The candidate demonstrates a thoughtful and detailed approach to the question and uses a range of valid points to explore Phil's character in the play. They examine the writer's methods and apply appropriate subject terminology.

They also include some thoughtful contextual references to support explanations.

Notional Mark: 23

Notional Grade: 6

Notional Level: 5

This page intentionally left blank

10

A Guide to Writing your Examination Answer

You will be given a choice between two questions – historically, one tends to be **about character** and the other tends to be **about a theme**.

Character question

When it's a character based question, try to discuss what their character is symbolic/representative of.

Introduce a line of argument: Kelly presents the idea that characters such as... are symbolic of... therefore...

Step 1
Then pick two adjectives to describe that character

From the offset Kelly presents Phil as being authoritative and decisive.

Step 2
Mention techniques and begin discussion

From Phil's dialogue we can see that he is very focused on a solution to the 'crime' and despite the panic of others, he remains in control, selecting his words carefully: 'Cathy, Danny, Mark, you go to Adam's house, you wait until his mum's out, you break in.'

Step 3
Analyze in as much detail at word level

The word/phrase... The use of the second-person pronoun, 'you', three times in the same sentence, reveals his precision of thought, with an economy of language. He omits any unnecessary conjunctions, in order to focus the other characters on the actions he wishes them to carry out. It is syndetic in structure.

Step 4
Reinforce your previous point with more evidence. Remember, your evidence can relate to other characters, not just the one that is named in the question.

This is also shown through Kelly's use of...

Step 5
Make a link to themes/ideas – what are Kelly's intentions?

Kelly deliberately introduces this character in this way because...he wants the audience to identify with the moral issues implied by his actions. Phil is the leader who represents the question posed by Kelly in the play, 'How far will we go to save the group?', and symbolizes the idea of sacrificing an individual for the group, with the resulting consequences. Try here to link back to your line of argument.

Repeat the above as many times as you can in 45 minutes

Question about theme

Same as above, except:

Step 1

**State that this theme
is most prominently
demonstrated through
the character(s) of...**

This page intentionally left blank

11

Glossary of Terms

A

act a division of a play

adjective a word used to describe a noun in more detail

adverb a word used to describe verbs, often ending in '-ly', such as 'swiftly'

argument a reasoned point of view

asyndetic the omission of conjunctions from sentence constructions in which they would normally be used – for example, 'I came, I saw, I conquered' (rather than 'I came, then I saw, then I conquered')

atmosphere the tone or mood of the text

audience a group of people who hear, watch or read something

authentic genuine, real, veritable, sharing a sense of actuality and lacking falsehood or misrepresentation

authority power or influence, often because of knowledge or expertise (*related adjective*: authoritative)

C

character a fictional person

colloquial conversational or chatty (*related noun*: colloquialism)

conclusion the end

conjunction a word such as 'and' or 'but' which is used to join two words, clauses or phrases, sentences or paragraphs

connotation a meaning that is suggested by the use of a word or phrase

content the subject matter; what something contains

context the circumstances

D

dialogue speech between two or more people; conversation

E

ellipses (...) punctuation indicating that something has been left out

emotive language the language used to provoke emotions in the reader or audience, such as shock or pity

evidence information used to support a point being made

expletives swear words, or other terms which could be considered offensive

explicit open, obvious

F

form a type of writing or the way it is presented

G

genre a kind or type of literature, for example, a detective story or romance, or a play

I

identify to select; to name

image a picture, also used metaphorically as 'word pictures'

imagery when words are so descriptive that they paint a picture in your mind. Imagery is used to allow the reader to empathize or imagine the moment being described

imply to suggest something that is not explicitly stated (*related noun*: implication; *related adjective*: implicit)

infer to deduce something that is not openly stated (*related noun*: inference)

informal language conversational language that is spoken between people who are usually familiar with one another

interpret to infer meaning from implicit information or ideas and explain what you have inferred (*related noun*: interpretation)

issue a subject being discussed

L

location place

linguistic features the scientific study of language and its structure

M

metaphor an image created by directly comparing one thing to another, for example, Leah's line to Phil (page 47): 'Your brain is entirely waffle, single-mindedly waffle and maybe a bit of jam.'

modal verb a verb that shows you the mood or state of another verb, for example, 'could' or 'might'

mood the general feeling conveyed (see also **atmosphere**)

morality ideas of good and bad behaviour, or right and wrong

motif an idea or image that is repeated at intervals in a text

motivation the reason(s) for doing something

N

noun a naming word

O

omission the missing out

opening start, beginning

opinion what someone thinks

P

period an amount of time

perspicacity shrewdness, acuity, astuteness, insight, acumen

perspective point of view

persuasive device persuasion is a literary technique that writers use to present their ideas through reasons and logic to influence the audience. Through persuasive devices, writers express their own feelings and opinions by appealing to the audience emotionally and rationally.

playwright a person who writes plays

plot the main events of a story

present tense the tense used to describe things happening now

probative providing proof or evidence

pronoun a short word which replaces a noun ('I', 'you', 'he', 'she', etc)

Q

quotation words or phrases taken directly from the text (*related verb*: to quote)

quotation marks inverted commas surrounding a quotation

R

repetition when words, phrases, ideas or sentences are used more than once, to highlight key issues and make important sections more memorable

rhetorical device a language technique used to influence an audience

rhetorical question a question that does not require an answer, used to make the reader think about the possible answer and involve them in the text

rhythm the beat of the writing, usually in poetry

S

scene a division of a play, often within an act

script the text of a play

setting where and when the action takes place

significance what something means or stands for

simile a figure of speech involving the comparison of one thing with another of a different kind, used to make a description more emphatic or vivid

simple sentence a sentence that only contains a main clause

slang informal language, often local and changing or evolving

social order where people are 'placed' in society, with some more important than others

speech marks inverted commas when used around direct speech

summarize to give a shortened account of something, retaining the meaning (*related noun*: summary)

symbol an object that represents something else, for example an idea or emotion (*related adjective*: symbolic)

syndetic connected by a conjunction

T

theme subject matter – what the text is about rather than what happens in it

third person he, she, it (singular); they (plural)

tone the overall feel or attitude of the writer

topic a sentence, usually the first in a paragraph, which tells you what the paragraph is about

tricolon a rhetorical term for a series of three parallel words, phrases or clauses

V

verb a doing, thinking, feeling or being word

view point of view

vocabulary the words used

voice the narrator or speaker; his or her characteristic style

This page intentionally left blank

12

Appendix

An Interview with Dennis Kelly (28 April 2016)

Students from Heath Park School, Wolverhampton, posed some questions for Dennis Kelly, and here are his responses.

Why did you select these three locations in the play?

Dennis Kelly: I selected the locations because I wanted the play to be cyclical so that we would keep coming back to the same place and each time there is a change because their world changes. They are in the world of having killed someone or believing they have. Then they are in the world of the lying and then they are in the world of the consequences of that lie. A field is quite a private place as you can see people coming from far away. The location is the same but the circumstances change. I wanted the locations to repeat. I also chose these locations because they were ones I recognized from my childhood, the woods, the street and the field.

We wondered why the character John Tate disappeared so soon in the play?

Dennis Kelly: I don't know why John Tate disappeared but I liked it – that happens sometimes, people drift away from our lives like a friend we may intend to keep in touch with but never do. His leaving without explanation tells us more about his psychological state than if he stayed. It is interesting in a way because we expect him to come back. I hate it if I get a note to say 'I think this is completely out of character' – that's when it's interesting and it's interesting when it's not explained. What makes it real sometimes is when it seems not normal.

Did you make any concessions because you were writing a play specifically for young people? Tell us about that.

Dennis Kelly: I made no concessions for writing for young people. I wrote this play as I wrote any play – I didn't water it down for young people, as young people are bright and they are sharp. We stay in the world of the children, but there is the world of the imagination beyond the play.

Kids like thinking and Leah is really profound when she talks about bonobos and chimps. When we first discovered chimps, we didn't know about bonobos 'cos they looked the same. Our narrative is that chimps are our nearest relatives, and they are more violent. Leah and her flights of fancy – it doesn't do any good but she likes to think and is really profound.

Young people like to think. Cathy is violent and she has an ability to be cruel. When we see Phil he is like a shadow in their world. Their world is different to the adult world. Kids always had to solve their own problems and the world of childhood can be terrifying. It may be different in school today – they have someone to speak to when they are being bullied. This play is not about bullying – the bullying has already happened.

What is your view of Phil in the play?

Dennis Kelly: My view of Phil – he has always been... – he just wants to stay out of it. He just thinks 'I've probably got 2 years of this' – he's shut down – food is simple as opposed to projecting all this crazy stuff – Leah just lets him. They enjoy each other's company. It outlines the event when Phil gets involved.

Tell us about your use of language in the play.

Dennis Kelly: Language is very incomplete and very rarely does it give us any information – it is not really the thing we are doing, we are like chimps picking fleas off each other. Language – it's all in the subtext. I am influenced by many writers like Edward Bond and Caryl Churchill [most influential].

When Leah refers to the stars and 'I mean stars, Phil, a billion nuclear reactions a second' and later when Richard replaces Leah in the field with Phil, and says 'I knew there was life in other planets', it suggests there is a world outside themselves which they imagine.

Dennis Kelly: Yes, otherwise it would just be like a soap opera. The bits in between such as Leah's monologues for example – without these it might have just been like a soap opera.

You were commissioned to write the play for young people, as part of the Connections Initiative of the National Theatre in 2008. Do you think this play *DNA* can be transferred to film or television?

Dennis Kelly: I don't think I could transfer this play *DNA* to film or television. Theatre feels very different – you can do psychologically detailed things in a play. [But he isn't sure that's right having said it, but it is clear that the theatre is his choice of genre for this play.]

Why did you write this play?

Dennis Kelly: It was really what was in my head at the time about group responsibility and the individual. The Iraq war and the July bombings in London, we were living in a climate of fear and we still are and it's getting worse, whenever these sorts of things happen we think about civil liberties and the threat to them. It is about the right to protect the good group. It's not about bullying – that has already happened before the play starts – it is more about consequences. Phil is not Machiavellian. When we try to solve problems with a lie it doesn't work. We went to war because Saddam Hussein is a bad man, but there are shades of grey in all of us as there are in people in the group. Phil is very outside the action.
I don't believe in good or bad. The question is: how far will we go to save the group? When I write a play I don't have an answer. I think about a question I don't have an answer to – there's never an easy answer as this makes it more interesting although the play does pose this moral question. Lying is a waste as human beings are machines for working things out.

13
Resources for Photocopying

Often, many of us find it helpful to think things through visually when we are thinking about putting a text on its feet. In this section we have provided a range of figures, an idea for stage blocks, so that you can copy these out and try the figures for any particular episode in the play. Trying out your ideas visually can really help you think about ways of interpreting the status of characters as well as the relationships between them. It can also help you think through possible motivations, for example if you decide they are seated or standing, facing or blocking others. Playing around with positions, while referring to textual episodes or particular lines helps you experiment with the script in a different way, before you come to your own interpretation.

USING THE DRAWINGS

A Note from Denise Jones, about using the following resources, in order to play around with interpretations of moments from the play and build your personal response

Seeing the play visually

Before I began teaching I worked as a theatre designer and model maker in the theatre. A designer creates costume drawings, technical drawings and a 1:25 scale model of the set. As part of the set, a few small figures are also made so that the director can get a feel of the scale and what it will look like when realized/ built. The director can also move the figures around the model to give him/her an idea of how to block the actors, where they might position particular characters to indicate their significance in the scene and to demonstrate the relationships between characters. This helps them experiment with ideas, to see the effect of seating characters or standing them, grouping them or isolating them, facing the audience or having their back to the audience, all of which helps them to interpret meaning. They might for example have a character on a lower level to show a difference of status. The model will also provide the director with a vision of the space the actors will be working in and the way that space is filled by the interaction between the actors. The director may choose to create a large space between characters, if they feel they are trying to avoid each other. They may decide, for example, that Phil turns away from Leah when she tries her best to communicate with him, when we first meet them in the location of the field, in Act 1, Scene 2.

Many other departments in the theatre use the model and drawings such as the construction department, costume, properties, paint shop etc. Plays are performed in a 3 dimensional world/space which is why the model is so important to so many people because that is how the audience will see it. When I think of a design, in my head I can imagine it from all angles because I am a visual learner. Some of you may work in this way too so you may find these resources useful. For those of you who are not visual learners, these will still be useful as they are tangible which means it doesn't require the need to think visually in your head, it's really there in front of you.

In order to help you visualize the play and interpret its meaning through a personal response this way of experimenting is really useful, as it will help YOU decide on YOUR interpretation, using sections of the play to interpret meaning in a very immediate and concrete way.

How you can use the resources to help you see the play visually and bring your personal interpretation to it

We have included some simple resources which can be used as the director might use a real set design. There are:

- Squares to represent rostra/stage blocks

- A simple ground plan including seating and some figures

- Figures

A model built for a play is of course normally entirely 3D, including chairs and rostra, but to keep things simple we have kept things in 2D, because your purpose is to use this theatrical device (as it is a play after all) in order to interpret your analysis of character and theme to meet the requirements of a literature examination. As you move the characters around you are implicitly considering your thoughts about those characters, and when you are positioning them you are also addressing themes such as power and hierarchy.

Print the figures and rostra onto thin card and enlarge the ground plan onto A3 paper or card. They will then both be 1:25 scale. This means they are 25 times smaller than real life.

Print and cut out as many figures as you need or you can draw your own the same size. Place onto a penny with some sticky tack. The figures are then easily picked up and moved around.

The rostra can be cut out as squares, oblongs or any suitable shape, and placed appropriately to represent, for example, a log, tree stump and so on. In the centre draw a circle with the height measurement inside i.e. 600 which would be millimetres high in reality. The height is important because the use of levels to represent for example, power and hierarchy needs to be something we can identify visually.

The basic theatre ground plan is one possibility but you could cut out the chairs and place them in whatever configuration you want, for example as theatre in the round, proscenium, thrust, promenade or any other configuration wish to consider. Play around with ideas until you feel comfortable with your final layout.

You may wish to photograph your ideas once you have designed a key moment from the play, and it can help you think through your ideas if you annotate your figures and setting, for example Phil stands and stares at the entire group to demonstrate his authority, during a pause at the moment when he instructs the others, 'Cathy, Danny, Mark, you go to Adam's house, you wait until his mum's out, you break in' (Act 1, Scene 3, Page 24).

What is happening when I am working on these tasks? How is this helping me revise?

As you move the characters around you are implicitly considering your thoughts about those characters, and when you are positioning them you are also addressing themes such as power and hierarchy. Your examination questions will focus on either characters or themes

5' 10"   Fig. 1   Fig. 2

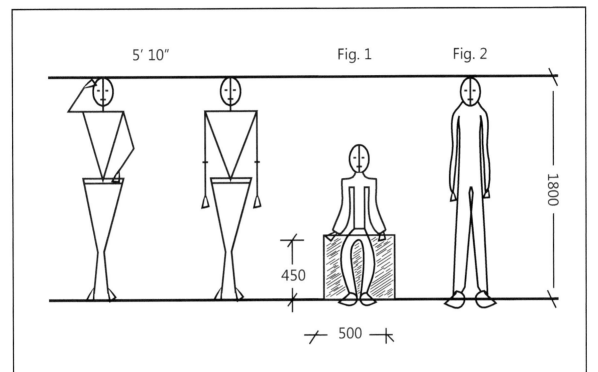

1800

450

500

Fig. 3

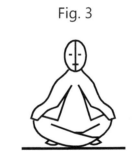

Scale 1:25mm

Copy and use Fig. 1, 2, 3 as many times as needed. Their height is approximately 5'10" or 180 cm tall. Place on a penny or 5p with blue tac after they have been photocopied onto card and cut out.

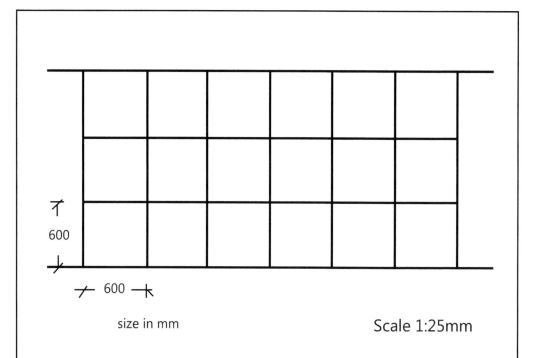

size in mm

Scale 1:25mm

Squares to represent stage blocks or set etc. The height can be written in a circle so students know how high they are from stage level.

1 metre etc.

Cut out and use as necessary.

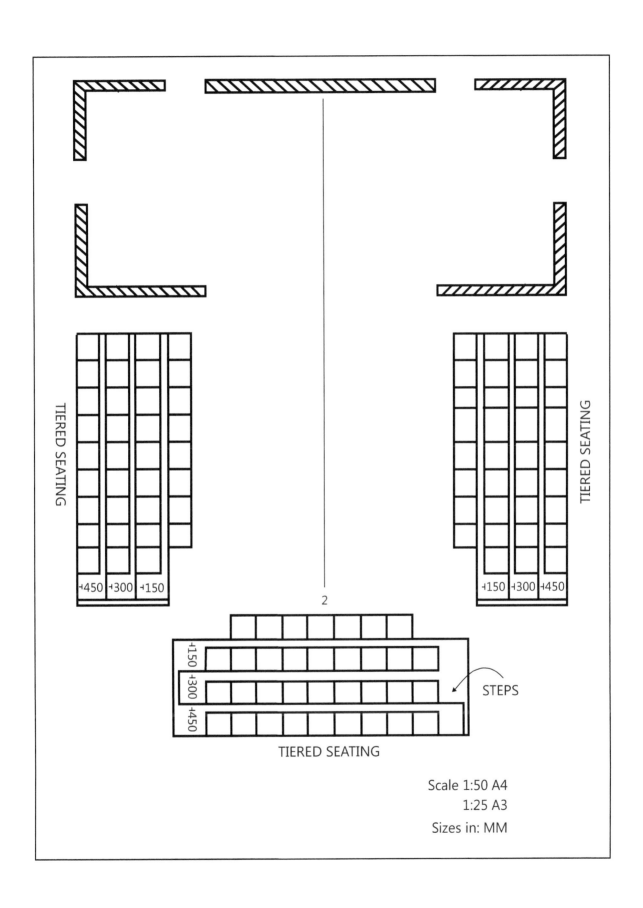

TIERED SEATING

TIERED SEATING

+450 +300 +150

+150 +300 +450

2

+150

+300

+450

STEPS

TIERED SEATING

Scale 1:50 A4

1:25 A3

Sizes in: MM

USING THE PHOTOGRAPHS

Some useful revision tasks

- Try sequencing the photographs in order as you think they may appear in the play. Then check against the play text or the summary in this revision guide to see if it makes sense to you.

- Now have a go at placing the quotes provided here against the photographs to see which you think makes more sense to you.

Jan and Mark

Jan and Mark

Leah and Phil

Phil, Danny, Cathy, Richard, Brian, Mark, Jan and Leah

Jan and Mark

Phil and Leah

Danny, Lou and Phil

Cathy

Brian, Jan and Mark

Phil, Leah, Lou, Danny, Richard, Jan, Mark and Brian

Phil, Leah, Lou, Danny, Richard, Jan, Mark and Brian

Cathy, Brian, Leah, Mark, Phil, Lou, Adam and Jan

Cathy, Brian, Leah, Mark, Phil, Lou, Adam and Jan

Cathy, Brian, Leah, Mark, Phil, Lou, Adam and Jan

Notes

Act 1, **Scene 1** (page 10)

Location: A Street

MARK: Dead.

JAN: Oh.

MARK: Yes.

JAN: God.

MARK: Yes.

JAN: God.

MARK: Exactly.

Pause.

JAN: What are we going to do?

Act 1, **Scene 1** (page 10)

Location: A Field

LEAH: What are you thinking?

No answer.

No, don't tell me, sorry, that's a stupid, that's such a stupid –

You can tell me, you know. You can talk to me.

Act 1, **Scene 3** (page 22)

Location: A Wood

JAN: I mean he was still joking all the way, but

MARK: you could tell

JAN: He weren't really

MARK: fear

JAN: well

Act 1, **Scene 3** (page 24)

Location: A Wood

PHIL: Cathy, Danny, Mark, you go to Adam's house, you wait until his mum's out, you break in

---

Act 2, **Scene 1** (page 30)

Location: A Street

JAN: That's what he said?

MARK: That's what he said, I'm saying that's what he said.

JAN: Shit.

MARK: Exactly.

Beat.

JAN: What are we going to do?

Act 2, **Scene 2** (page 32)

Location: A Field

LEAH: What have we done, Phil?

Act 2, **Scene 3** (page 34)

Location: A Wood

DANNY: What are we gonna do?

LOU: We're screwed.

Act 2, **Scene 3** (page 38)

Location: A Wood

CATHY: Well, we thought, you know, I mean you'd given a description so we thought, well, I thought, you know, show initiative, we'll look for a fat balding postman with bad teeth.

Act 2, **Scene 3** (page 39)

Location: A Wood

BRIAN: I'm not going to the police station.

JAN: He has to. They're looking for him.

Act 2, **Scene 3** (page 39)

Location: A Wood

BRIAN: I can't go in. It was bad enough talking to them before, saying what I said, but I can't do it again.

Act 2, **Scene 3** (page 39)

Location: A Wood

BRIAN: I can't face it. They look at me. They look at me like I'm lying and it makes me cry. I can't stand the way they look at me. And then, because I cry, they think I'm telling the truth, but I'm crying because I'm lying and I feel terrible inside.

Act 3, **Scene 3** (page 52)

Location: A Wood

JAN: What are we gonna do?

Act 3, **Scene 3** (page 52)

Location: A Wood

LEAH: What happened.

ADAM doesn't answer.

Act 3, **Scene 3** (page 52)

Location: A Wood

LEAH: Phil?

What are we gonna...?

Phil?

Phil?

Say something Phil!

Pause. But PHIL says nothing.

Dimension Chart

Step 1	Step 2	Step 3
Initial Observations	**Textual Evidence**	**Inferences we can make from evidence**

What I think about   **Inferences**

... is He is often...		
He is one of the few characters... He is concerned about...		

Dimension Chart

Step 1	Step 2	Step 3
Initial Observations	Textual Evidence	Inferences we can make from evidence

What I think about...   **Inferences**

... is **She is often...**		
She is one of the few characters... **She is concerned about...**		

Dimension Chart

Step 1	Step 2	Step 3
Initial Observations	Textual Evidence	Inferences we can make from evidence

What I think about		Inferences
... is **He is often...**		
He is one of the few characters... **He is concerned about...**		

Dimension Chart

Step 1	Step 2	Step 3
Initial Observations	Textual Evidence	Inferences we can make from evidence

What I think about...

Inferences

... is

She is often...

She is one of the few characters...

She is concerned about...

Iona Towler-Evans is a National Trainer in teaching and learning, who contributes regularly to national and international teaching and learning conferences. She ran a successful English department in a school in challenging circumstances, and took on the role of Deputy Head. She is currently co-authoring a book on pedagogy, *Imagining to Learn* with Professor Brian Edmiston (Ohio State University) and Dr Viv Aitken (New Zealand). She has fulfilled roles as adviser and Inspector of English, and is currently both on the executive board of the NATD (National Association of Teachers of Drama) and a governor of Woodrow School in Worcestershire. She regularly publishes articles on practice, contributes to teaching and learning within English departments, and is currently contributing to the Lead Creative School Scheme in Wales.

This revision guide has drawn on the significant contribution of **Carl Eastwood**, a teacher of English who has successfully taught AQA, since its inception. During his 22-year career, he has taught successfully at a range of schools, including those in challenging circumstances. He is currently teacher of English in a highly successful English department, at the prestigious Old Swinford Hospital School, Stourbridge, in the West Midlands. Carl has been a long standing colleague of Iona's and they are currently embarking on an extended research project into classroom engagement.

Denise Jones is an experienced secondary school teacher of Art and Drama, and, as a theatre designer, has experimented with iconic approaches to learning, particularly in theatre. Based on the play *DNA* by Dennis Kelly, Denise devised a series of tasks for students to consider as part of their study and revision, and these successful ideas are included in this revision guide. Denise has also collaborated with Iona on numerous teaching and learning programmes for many years, as well as articles for the *Gifted and Talented Magazine*.

We acknowledge the enthusiastic contribution of **Caroline Wilkes**, MA Teacher of Drama at Heath Park School, Wolverhampton and her successful GCSE Year 11 **Drama students** (July 2016), for trialling the contents of this revision guide and providing photographs for the tasks included.

We are grateful to **Dennis Kelly**, the playwright for generously giving his time to respond to the students' questions about the play.